The Six Dharma Gates To the Sublime

The publication of this book has been enabled by
a generous donation from Upāsaka Guo Ke.

A Note on the Proper Care of Dharma Materials

Traditional Buddhist cultures treat books on Dharma as sacred. Hence it is considered disrespectful to place them in a low position, to read them when lying down, or to place them where they might be damaged by food or drink.

The Six Dharma Gates To the Sublime

A Classic Meditation Manual On Traditional Indian Buddhist Meditation

By the Great Tiantai Meditation Master & Exegete
Śramaṇa Zhiyi (Chih-i)
(538–597 CE)

Translation by Bhikshu Dharmamitra

Kalavinka Press
Seattle, Washington
WWW.KALAVINKAPRESS.ORG

KALAVINKA PRESS
8603 39th Ave SW
Seattle, WA 98136 USA

WWW.KALAVINKAPRESS.ORG / WWW.KALAVINKA.ORG

Kalavinka Press is the publishing arm of the Kalavinka Dharma Association, a non-profit organized exclusively for religious educational purposes as allowed within the meaning of section 501(c)3 of the Internal Revenue Code. KDA was founded in 1990 and gained formal approval in 2004 by the United States Internal Revenue Service as a 501(c)3 non-profit organization to which donations are tax deductible.

Donations to KDA are accepted by mail and on the Kalavinka website where numerous free Dharma translations and excerpts from Kalavinka publications are available in digital format.

Edition: SGS-SA-0808-1.0

ISBN: 978-1-935413-01-1
Library of Congress Control Number: 2009920869

PUBLISHER'S CATALOGING-IN-PUBLICATION DATA

Zhiyi (Chih-i), 538–597.

[Liu miao fa men. English translation.]
The Six Dharma Gates to the Sublime. A Classic Meditation Manual on Traditional Indian Buddhist Meditation.

Translated by Bhikshu Dharmamitra. – 1st ed. – Seattle, WA: Kalavinka Press, 2009.

p. ; cm.
ISBN: 978-1-935413-01-1
Includes: text outline; facing-page Chinese source text in both traditional and simplified scripts; notes.

1. Tiantai Buddhism – Doctrines – Early works to 1800. 2. Meditation – Tiantai Buddhism – Early works to 1800. 3. Śamatha (Buddhism) – Early works to 1800. 4. Vipaśyanā (Buddhism) – Early works to 1800. I. Title.

2009920869
0902

Cover and interior designed and composed by Bhikshu Dharmamitra.

Dedicated to the memory of the selfless and marvelous life of the Venerable Dhyāna Master Hsuan Hua, the Weiyang Ch'an Patriarch and the very personification of the Bodhisattva Path.

Dhyāna Master Hsuan Hua

宣化禪師

1918–1995

Acknowledgments

The accuracy and readability of of these first ten books of translations have been significantly improved with the aid of extensive corrections, preview comments, and editorial suggestions generously contributed by Bhikkhu Bodhi, Jon Babcock, Timothy J. Lenz, Upasaka Feng Ling, Upāsaka Guo Ke, Upāsikā Min Li, and Richard Robinson. Additional valuable editorial suggestions and corrections were offered by Bhikshu Huifeng and Bruce Munson.

The initial publication and short-run printing of the initial set of ten translation volumes have been assisted by substantial donations to the Kalavinka Dharma Association by Bill and Peggy Brevoort, Freda Chen, David Fox, Upāsaka Guo Ke, Chenping and Luther Liu, Sunny Lou, Jimi Neal, and "Leo L." (*Camellia sinensis folium*). Additional donations were offered by Doug Adams, Diane Hodgman, Bhikshu Huifeng, Joel and Amy Lupro, Richard Robinson, Ching Smith, and Sally and Ian Timm.

Were it not for the ongoing material support provided by my late guru's Dharma Realm Buddhist Association and the serene translation studio provided by Seattle's Bodhi Dhamma Center, creation of this translation would have been immensely more difficult.

Most importantly, it would have been impossible for me to produce this translation without the Dharma teachings provided by my late guru, the Weiyang Ch'an Patriarch, Dharma teacher, and exegete, the Venerable Master Hsuan Hua.

Citation and Romanization Protocols

Kalavinka Press *Taisho* citation style adds text numbers after volume numbers and before page numbers to assist rapid CBETA digital searches.

Romanization, where used, is Pinyin with the exception of names and terms already well-recognized in Wade-Giles.

The Chinese Text

This translation is supplemented by inclusion of Chinese source text on verso pages in both traditional and simplified scripts. Taisho-supplied variant readings from other editions are presented as Chinese endnotes.

This Chinese text and its variant readings are from the April, 2004 version of the Chinese Buddhist Electronic Text Association's digital edition of the Taisho compilation of the Buddhist canon.

Those following the translation in the Chinese should be aware that Taisho scripture punctuation is not traceable to original editions, is often erroneous and misleading, and is probably best ignored altogether. (In any case, accurate reading of Classical Chinese does not require any punctuation at all.)

General Table of Contents

Directory to Chapter Subsections

Introduction

The Nature of the Text and the Rationale for Translating It

The Six Dharma Gates to the Sublime is a 1500-year-old Buddhist meditation manual devoted to explaining the practice of calming-and-insight meditation according to a classic Indian Buddhist formula known as "the six gates." Although the actual content of this meditation practice formula is not confined to either Southern or Northern traditions, it is presented herein from a distinctly mahāyānistic standpoint assuming and encouraging bodhisattva path practice and the resolve to realize buddhahood.

Although I had long been aware of the existence of this text, I had never taken the time to study it closely and reflect upon its contents until I happened to be driving up the Oregon coast in the summer of 2001. I recall pulling over at an ocean overlook north of Newport, slowly reading it, and then deciding then and there to translate it. Consequently, I did just that, stopping at a rest stop and translating day-and-night for a few days, taking occasional brief breaks to stare out at the ocean or walk on the beach. Having finished the first draft, I then drove on back to Seattle with what I considered to be the perfect companion volume to my early-nineties translation of Master Zhiyi's *Essentials for Practicing Calming-and-Insight and Dhyāna Meditation*. Indeed, these two short calming-and-insight meditation works by Master Zhiyi are closely related in content, so much so that the original-language editions are often bound together into a single volume to facilitate simultaneous study and reference.

I recall feeling at the time that this work could serve the Western Dharma community as an important resource for better understanding what is contained within the purview of "calming-and-insight" (*śamatha-vipaśyanā*) meditation practice. It seems particularly useful to release both of these meditation translations at this time when English-language meditation instruction is still generally not so very broad in its scope, and not so very deep in its profundity. In fact, as of this writing, it seems more the norm than the exception that Western Buddhists do not necessarily even understand or believe in the fact of reincarnation, and beyond that, are often more predisposed to use meditation practice as a means to pleasurably adapt to karma-bound worldly existence than to use it as a means to transcend domination by mundane priorities. My hope in publishing these meditation manual translations is that at least some small sector of serious Western Dharma practitioners will have yet more textual bases for realizing the greater aims of Buddhist meditation which indeed do go beyond the mere allaying of the angsts of day-to-day afflictions in the present lifetime.

The Relationship of This Text to Other Zhiyi Meditation Texts

The Six Gates to the Sublime is one of four "calming-and-insight" meditation texts written by the illustrious Tiantai meditation master and exegete, Master Zhiyi (538–597 CE): In his preface to *Essentials for Practicing Calming-and-Insight and Dhyāna Meditation,* the Song Dynasty monk Yuanzhao describes the four meditation texts written by that famous meditation master:

> There are four "calming-and-insight" texts in the Tiantai tradition:
>
> The first, known as the "perfect and sudden" (*The Great Calming and Contemplation*) was presented in the form of lectures by the Great Master at Yuquan ("Jade Spring") Monastery in Jingzhou Prefecture. Zhang'an (章安) transcribed it in ten fascicles.
>
> The second, known as the "gradual and sequential," was lectured at Waguan ("Tiled House") Monastery. Disciple Fashen (法慎) transcribed it. Originally comprising thirty fascicles, Zhang'an edited it into ten fascicles. It is what is known today as *The Dhyāna Pāramitā.*
>
> The third, known as the "unfixed," is the one which the Chen Dynasty Chief State Secretary (尚書令), Maoxi (毛喜), requested the Great Master to issue. It consists of a single fascicle known today as *The Six Gates to the Sublime.*
>
> The fourth, known as *The Smaller Calming-and-Insight* [or *The Essentials for Practicing Calming-and-Insight and Dhyāna Meditation*]… was brought forth by the Great Master for his elder brother, Chenzhen. Truly, it is a condensation of the large edition and a presentation of the very crux of the means for entering the Path. (T46.1915.462a)

The Potential Usefulness of This Text for Western Buddhism

Of those four meditation texts described above, this present volume is the third, whereas my previously-translated *The Essentials for Practicing Calming-and-Insight and Dhyāna Meditation* is the fourth. Of the two texts, *The Essentials* is marvelously complete, describing virtually anything one would need to know to practice meditation correctly while also dealing effectively with any problems which might arise. Yuanzhao's judgment that it is in effect a condensation of Master Zhiyi's encyclopedically-complete *Great Calming-and-Contemplation* is indicative of its comprehensiveness.

This *Six Gates* text, however, greatly expands the breadth of our view and the depth of our understanding of what is actually involved in carrying on a mature "calming-and-insight" meditation practice. These qualities make it especially useful to the meditator who finds that his practice is "stuck" and does not show any particular advancement beyond the development of a light easefulness helpful in damping down the intensity of day-to-day mental afflictions. It is in this sense that the present text may be especially useful as an adjunct meditation text complementing its companion volume, *The Essentials for Practicing Calming-and-Insight and Dhyāna Meditation*.

Both of these texts, being relatively short and straightforward, are particularly well suited for Western Dharma practitioners devoted to serious cultivation of Buddhist meditation.

Textual History of Six-Gates "Calming-and-Insight" Practice

The "six gates" are: counting, following, stabilization, contemplation, turning, and purification. The "sublime" (*praṇīta*) of *The Six Gates to the Sublime* is a deliberate reference to the third of the four practice-aspects of the third of the four truths of the ārya, the truth of cessation (*nirodha*). (See note 11, page 143.)

Master Zhiyi attributes the historical basis for six-gates calming-and-insight meditation to Shakyamuni Buddha's reliance upon this method as he sat beneath the bodhi tree and gained the utmost, right, and perfect enlightenment in Sixth Century BCE India. To support this conclusion, he cites the detailed testimony to that effect in the *Origins Sutra on the Prince's Auspicious Response* (太子瑞應本起經 / T02.185.476c), a sutra translated from Sanskrit into Chinese by Zhiqian between 223 and 253 CE, quoting that scripture as follows:

> He directed his thought inwardly to *ānāpāna* (meditation on the breath): first, counting (*gaṇanā*); second, following (*anugamaḥ*); third, stabilization (*sthānam*), fourth, contemplation (*upalakṣaṇā*); fifth, turning (*vivartanā*); and sixth, purification (*pariśuddhiḥ*). (These parenthetically-included Sanskrit antecedents for the six gates are as recorded in De la Valleé Poussin's translation of *L'Abhidharmakośa de Vasubandhu*.)

Further testimony for the early Indian history of this formula for engaging calming-and-insight practice is found in numerous locations in the Canon, for instance:

1) This same six-component formula is explained in precisely the same order in the *Abhidharma Vibhāṣā* of Kātyāyaniputra, an author dating to roughly 200 BCE (阿毘曇毘婆沙 / T28.1546.105b29–6a01).

2) The identically named and listed formula is also discussed at yet greater length in the *Mahā-vibhāṣā* of Vasumitra, an author dating to roughly 50 BCE (阿毘達磨大毘婆沙論 / T27.1545.134c26–5b20)

3) The formula is also treated in the early Fourth Century CE by Vasubandhu in his *Abhidharma-kośa-bhāṣyam.* (See the Leo Pruden translation, pp. 922–3.)

4) Pruden refers us in turn to two Pali scripture locations: *Dīgha,* ii.291; *Majjhima,* i.425 (p. 1049, note 89).

5) Finally, Buddhaghosa's later Pali-tradition commentary preserves the same list in an only slightly altered version, the sole differences being that one additional element is interpolated ("touching"), whilst "reviewing" is tacked on at the end as an eighth member of the list (*Path of Purification,* VIII: 189-225, p. 300-309). So we can see that Buddhaghosa in fact presents us with a modified version of the same list. Not too surprising, as he is the latest of these authors.

As a consequence of reviewing the above, it should be clear to the reader that we deal here with a calming-and-insight meditation-instruction formula traditional in the very earliest period of Indian Buddhism. Hence there is no historical basis for concluding that, because the author is Chinese, the content is somehow typical of the priorities of Sino-Buddhist meditation traditions. That said, a seriously-engaged meditation practice linked to careful study of both *The Essentials for Practicing Calming-and-Insight and Dhyāna Meditation* and *The Six Gates to the Sublime* will lead one to the inescapable conclusion that Ch'an is just a radical and sudden approach to perfecting all of the aspects of calming-and-insight practice described in those texts. In short, in terms of aims, essence, and results, the two approaches to awakening are, in the final analysis, not different at all.

The Doctrinal Content of this Text

As any student of Indian Buddhist meditation will certainly know, the essence of meditation practice lies in balanced development of the two fundamental endeavors of achieving the deep and wakeful mental stillness of "calming" (*śamatha*) on the one hand and the wisdom realizations of analytic "insight" contemplation (*vipaśyanā*) on the other. The "six gates" (counting, following, stabilization, contemplation, turning, and purification) constitute a practice formula for achieving precisely those ends.

The manner in which these six techniques are actually employed in one's meditation practice is not fixed. It may indeed be the case that one takes up these six practice techniques in a strictly serial sequence, beginning with the "counting" of the breaths as in standard *ānāpāna* breath-meditation practice and progressing on toward "purification." However, where circumstances call for a less straightforward application of the techniques, they may instead be appropriately applied as required at each of the various levels of meditative absorption, may be employed as precisely tailored responses to the exigencies of individual circumstances, or may be employed as counteractive antidotes to specific hindrances interfering with meditative progress.

The text goes on to describe further permutations of the different ways in which the six techniques may be understood and may be applied. A slow and reflective reading of the text will allow the deeper meaning of the six gates to become more directly perceptible to the individual practitioner. The reader is encouraged to give particularly close attention to the implications of the later chapters starting with the "reversed" practice which turns back its focus on the emptiness of all phenomena to treat the implications involved in bodhisattva practice of the Path. Following on that chapter, we have the equally fascinating and useful chapters on "contemplation of mind," "perfect contemplation," and "signs of realization."

In Summation

As noted above, I first produced a preliminary draft of this translation in 2001. Owing to the importance of the work, I have allowed various copyrighted provisional drafts to be posted on Kalavinka websites since then. Because the present version of the translation is immensely improved in accuracy over previous versions, it should in all cases be preferred as the definitive edition. It gives me great pleasure to be able to introduce such a potentially beneficial meditation text into the world of Western Buddhism, not least because confusion about right meditation practice is still so very widespread.

I would like to express particular gratitude to those who have reviewed the Chinese and English of the text, pointing out problems in earlier drafts of this work.

Due to the terseness of the language and the abstruseness of the concepts and practices treated, it is inevitable that there will be room for further refinement of aspects of this translation. I hope that any specialists or practitioners encountering such infelicities will favor me with recommendations for improvement, forwarding them via the Kalavinka Press website.

I especially hope that Buddhist practitioners may find this text useful in development of meditation practice and in advancement on the Path.

Bhikshu Dharmamitra
Seattle, January 2nd, 2008

The Six Dharma Gates To the Sublime

六妙法門

By Śramaṇa Zhiyi (Chih-i)
From Tiantai Mountain's Dhyāna Cultivation Monastery
天台山修禪寺沙門智顗述

Translation by Bhikshu Dharmamitra

No. 1917

六妙法门

天台大师于都下瓦官寺略出此法门

[0549a06] 六妙门者。盖是内行之根本。三乘得道之要迳。故释迦初诣道树。跏趺坐草。内思安般。一数。二随。三止。四观五还。六净。因此万行开发。降魔成道。当知佛为物轨示迹若斯。三乘正士。岂不同游此路。所言六者。即是数法。约数明禅。故言六也。如佛或约一数辩禅。所谓一行三昧。或约二数。谓一止。二观。或约三数。谓三三昧。或约四数。所谓四禅。或约五数。谓五门禅。或约六数。谓六妙门。或约七数。谓七依定。或约八数。谓八背舍。或约九数。谓

简体字

No. 1917

六妙法門

天台大師於都下瓦官寺略出此法門

[0549a06] 六妙門者。蓋是內行之根本。三乘得道之要逕。故釋迦初詣道樹。跏趺坐草。內思安般。一數。二隨。三止。四觀五還。六淨。因此萬行開發。降魔成道。當知佛為物軌示跡若斯。三乘正士。豈不同遊此路。所言六者。即是數法。約數明禪。故言六也。如佛或約一數辯禪。所謂一行三昧。或約二數。謂一止。二觀。或約三數。謂三三昧。或約四數。所謂四禪。或約五數。謂五門禪。或約六數。謂六妙門。或約七數。謂七依定。或約八數。謂八背捨。或約九數。謂

正體字

The Six Dharma Gates to the Sublime[1]

The Great Master of Tiantai Mountain set forth these Dharma gates in this summary form at the Capital's Waguan Monastery.

Dhyāna Master Zhiyi's Preface

As for the "six gates to the sublime (*praṇīta*)," they constitute the very root of one's internal practice and the essential route to realization of the paths of the Three Vehicles.[2] Hence, when Shākyamuni first arrived at the Bodhi Tree[3] and sat down in lotus posture on the cushion of grass, "He directed his thought inwardly to *ānāpāna*:[4] first, counting (*gaṇanā*); second, following (*anugamaḥ*); third, stabilization (*sthānam*), fourth, contemplation (*upalakṣaṇā*); fifth, turning (*vivartanā*); and sixth, purification (*pariśuddhiḥ*)."[5] It was because of this that the myriad practices[6] opened forth and took effect, resulting in the subduing of the demons and the realization of the Path.

One should realize that the Buddha is the model for beings. Since he pointed out his own tracks in this fashion, how then could the orthodox personages of the Three Vehicles fail to all travel together along this road?

As for the "six," it is simply a dharma of enumeration. One explains dhyāna meditation by resort to a numerical formula. Hence we refer here to "six." This is just as when the Buddha sometimes discoursed on dhyāna according to a singular enumeration, namely the so-called "single-practice" samādhi, or did so according to a two-fold enumeration, namely first, calming (*śamatha*), and second, insight (*vipaśyanā*).

Sometimes he explained according to a threefold enumeration, namely the three samādhis. Sometimes, it was according to a four-fold enumeration, specifically, according to the four dhyānas. Sometimes it was according to a five-fold enumeration, the so-called "five-gate" dhyāna.[7] Sometimes, it was according to a six-fold enumeration, namely these six gates to the sublime. Sometimes, it was according to a seven-fold enumeration, the so-called "seven dependable absorptions."[8] Sometimes, it was according to an eight-fold enumeration, namely the eight liberations (*vimokṣa*). Sometimes, it was according to a nine-fold enumeration, namely according to

简体字	正體字
九次第定。或约十数。谓十禅支。如是等。乃至百千万亿阿僧只不可说诸三昧门。悉是约数说诸禅也。虽数有多少。穷其法相。莫不悉相收摄。以众生机悟不同故。有增减之数分别利物。今言六者。即是约数法而标章也。妙者其意乃多。若论正意。即是灭谛涅盘。故灭四行中。言灭止妙离。涅盘非断非常。有而难契。无而易得。故言妙也。六法能通。故名为门。门虽有六。会妙不殊故经言泥洹真法宝。众生从种种门入。此则通释六妙门之大意也。六妙门大意有十	九次第定。或約十數。謂十禪支。如是等。乃至百千萬億阿僧祇不可說諸三昧門。悉是約數說諸禪也。雖數有多少。窮其法相。莫不悉相收攝。以眾生機悟不同故。有增減之數分別利物。今言六者。即是約數法而標章也。妙者其意乃多。若論正意。即是滅諦涅槃。故滅四行中。言滅止妙離。涅槃非斷非常。有而難契。無而易得。故言妙也。六法能通。故名為門。門雖有六。會妙不殊故經言泥洹真法寶。眾生從種種門入。此則通釋六妙門之大意也。六妙門大意有十
[0549a27] 第一历别对诸禅六妙门　第二次第相生六妙门　第三随便宜六妙门	**[0549a27]** 第一歷別對諸禪六妙門　第二次第相生六妙門　第三隨便宜六妙門

the nine sequential absorptions.[9] Sometimes, it was according to a ten-fold enumeration, namely according to the ten branches of dhyāna.[10] In a manner such as this, it may reach even to a hundred thousand myriads of *koṭīs* of *asaṃkyeyas* of indescribably numerous gateways to samādhi.

All of these are instances of discussing the dhyānas according to numerical categories. Although the numerical categories may be either greater or lesser in number, when one exhausts all of the characteristic aspects of these dharmas, not a one of them fails to be mutually subsumed by the others. It is because of differences in the teaching opportunities presented by different beings and the differences in their levels of awakening that there is this increase and decrease in numerical discriminations set forth for their benefit.

Now, when we speak of "six," it is simply a case of using a dharma of enumeration to title the topics discussed. As for "sublime" (*praṇīta*), its meanings are numerous. If one wishes to discuss its orthodox primary meaning, it is just the nirvāṇa associated with the truth of cessation. Hence, among the four "practice-aspects" associated with [the truth of] cessation, we speak of: cessation (*nirodha*); tranquility (*śānta*); the sublime (*praṇīta*); and abandonment (*niḥsaraṇa*).[11] It is not the case that "nirvāṇa" involves either an instance of "cutting off" or an instance of "permanence." Though it might be [conceived of as] "existent," it would thus be a difficult thing to mesh with. Though it might be [conceived of as] "non-existent," it would thus be more easily realized. Hence it is described as "sublime."

Because these six dharmas facilitate one's ability to penetrate on through, they are therefore referred to as "gates." Although there are six of these gates, they are no different in their ability to facilitate one's encounter with the sublime. Thus the scriptures declare, "As for nirvāṇa, the true Dharma jewel, beings enter it through many different gates."[12]

This is but a general explanation of the greater meaning of the six gates to the sublime. This treatment of the greater meaning of the six gates to the sublime shall consist of ten sections:

1. The six gates to the sublime in relation to the dhyāna absorptions.
2. The six gates to the sublime in terms of sequential development.
3. The six gates to the sublime in accordance with suitability.

简体字	正體字
第四随对治六妙门　第五相摄六妙门　第六通别六妙门　第七旋转六妙门　第八观心六妙门　第九圆观六妙门　第十证相六妙门	第四隨對治六妙門　第五相攝六妙門　第六通別六妙門　第七旋轉六妙門　第八觀心六妙門　第九圓觀六妙門　第十證相六妙門

4. The six gates to the sublime as means of counteraction.
5. The six gates to the sublime in terms of mutual inclusion.
6. The six gates to the sublime in terms of identities and differences. **[549b]**
7. The six gates to the sublime in accordance with the "reversed" orientation.
8. The six gates to the sublime according to contemplation of the mind.
9. The six gates to the sublime according to the perfect contemplation.
10. The six gates to the sublime in accordance with the signs of realization.

简体字	正體字
[0549b03] 释第一历别对诸禅定明六妙门。即为六意。一者依数为妙门。行者因数息故。即能出生四禅。四无量心。四无色定。若于最后非非想定。能觉知非是涅盘。是人必定得三乘道。何以故。此定阴界入和合故有。虚诳不实。虽无麁烦恼。而亦成就十种细烦恼。知已破折不住不着。心得解脱。即证三乘涅盘故。此义如须跋陀罗。佛教断非非想处惑。即便获得阿罗汉果。数为妙门。意在于此也。二者随为妙门者。行者因随息故。即能出生十六特胜。所谓一知息入。二知息出。三知息长短。	**[0549b03]** 釋第一歷別對諸禪定明六妙門。即為六意。一者依數為妙門。行者因數息故。即能出生四禪。四無量心。四無色定。若於最後非非想定。能覺知非是涅槃。是人必定得三乘道。何以故。此定陰界入和合故有。虛誑不實。雖無麁煩惱。而亦成就十種細煩惱。知已破折不住不著。心得解脫。即證三乘涅槃故。此義如須跋陀羅。佛教斷非非想處惑。即便獲得阿羅漢果。數為妙門。意在於此也。二者隨為妙門者。行者因隨息故。即能出生十六特勝。所謂一知息入。二知息出。三知息長短。

Chapter One

The Six Gates in Relation to the Dhyāna Absorptions

I. The Six Gates in Relation to the Dhyāna Absorptions

There are six associated concepts here, as follows:

A. Counting

First, "counting" as a gate to the sublime: Through relying on counting the breaths, the practitioner gains the ability to manifest the four dhyānas, the four immeasurable minds, and the four formless absorptions. Upon reaching the very last one, the one known as the "neither perception nor non-perception" absorption, so long as he remains aware that [this absorption] does not qualify as nirvāṇa, this person will definitely be able to gain realization in the paths of the Three Vehicles.

How might this be so? This absorption exists on account of a conjunction of the aggregates, the sense realms, and the sense bases. It is false, deceptive, and unreal. Although one remains free of the coarse afflictions [in this absorption], still, one has nonetheless developed ten types of subtle afflictions. If, having realized this, one analyzes the situation so that one does not continue to abide therein and does not become attached to it, one's mind will succeed in gaining liberation and one will straightaway gain realization of the nirvāṇa associated with the Three Vehicles.

This concept is illustrated by the case of Subhadra: The Buddha taught him to sever the delusions inherent in the station of neither perception nor non-perception. Consequently he gained the realization of the fruit of arhatship. As for the ability of "counting" to serve as a "gate to the sublime," the conceptual basis for it resides in this.

B. Following

Second, "following" as a gate to the sublime: On account of following the breath, the practitioner becomes able to manifest the sixteen superior phenomena, namely:

1. Awareness that the breath is entering.
2. Awareness that the breath is exiting.
3. Awareness that the breath is long or short.

简体字	正體字
四知息遍身。五除诸身行。六心爰喜。七心受乐。八受诸心行。九心作喜。十心作摄。十一心作解脱。十二观无常。十三观出散。十四观离欲。十五观灭。十六观弃舍。云何观弃舍。此观破非想处惑。所以者何。凡夫修非想时。观有常处如痈如疮。观无想处如痴也。第一妙定名曰非想。作是念已。即弃舍有想无想。名非有想非无想。故知非想即是两舍之义。今佛弟子观行破折。义如前说。是故深观弃舍。不着非想能得涅盘。随为妙门。意在此也。三者止为妙门者。行者因止心故。即便次第发五轮禅。	四知息遍身。五除諸身行。六心爰喜。七心受樂。八受諸心行。九心作喜。十心作攝。十一心作解脫。十二觀無常。十三觀出散。十四觀離欲。十五觀滅。十六觀棄捨。云何觀棄捨。此觀破非想處惑。所以者何。凡夫修非想時。觀有常處如癰如瘡。觀無想處如癡也。第一妙定名曰非想。作是念已。即棄捨有想無想。名非有想非無想。故知非想即是兩捨之義。今佛弟子觀行破折。義如前說。是故深觀棄捨。不著非想能得涅槃。隨為妙門。意在此也。三者止為妙門者。行者因止心故。即便次第發五輪禪。

4. Awareness that the breath permeates the body.
5. Relinquishing all physical actions.
6. The mental experience of joy.
7. The mental experience of bliss.
8. The experiencing of all mental actions.
9. The mental production of joy.
10. The mental development of concentration.
11. The mental generation of liberation.
12. The contemplation of impermanence.
13. The contemplation of dispersion.
14. The contemplation of abandonment of desire.
15. The contemplation of cessation.
16. The contemplation of renunciation.

What is meant here by "the contemplation of renunciation"? This contemplation demolishes the delusions inherent in the station of neither perception nor non-perception. How is this the case? When the common person cultivates the station of neither perception nor non-perception, he looks upon the stations "possessed of thought"[1] as being like a boil or as being like an open wound, looks upon the station devoid of thought as being like stupidity, and looks upon the station of neither perception nor non-perception as the foremost sublime absorption. After he has had this thought, he then relinquishes both having thought and not having thought. This then is the basis of [the station of] "neither perception nor non-perception." One should realize therefore that [the station of] "neither perception nor non-perception" inherently involves the concept of a two-fold relinquishment.

Now, as for the analysis employed in contemplative practice by the disciples of the Buddha, the concept is as discussed above. Therefore they engage in a deep contemplation, exercise renunciation, and refrain from becoming attached to the station of neither perception nor non-perception. Consequently, they are able to achieve realization of nirvāṇa. As for the ability of "following" to serve as a gate to the sublime, the conceptual basis abides in this.

C. Stabilization

Third, "stabilization" (*sthānam*) as a gate to the sublime: On account of stabilizing the mind, the practitioner then generates in sequence the "five-wheel" dhyānas,[2] as follows:

简体字	正體字
一者地轮三昧。即未到	一者地輪三昧。即未到
地。二者水轮三昧。即是	地。二者水輪三昧。即是
种种诸禅定善根发也。三	種種諸禪定善根發也。三
者虚空轮三昧。即五方便	者虛空輪三昧。即五方便
人觉因缘无性如虚空。四	人覺因緣無性如虛空。四
者金沙轮三昧。即是见思	者金沙輪三昧。即是見思
解脱。无着正惠如金沙	解脫。無著正惠如金沙
也。五者金刚轮三昧。即	也。五者金剛輪三昧。即
是第九无碍道。能断三界	是第九無礙道。能斷三界
结使。永尽无馀。证尽智	結使。永盡無餘。證盡智
无生智入涅盘。止为妙	無生智入涅槃。止為妙
门。意在此也。四者观为	門。意在此也。四者觀為
妙门者。行者因修观故。	妙門者。行者因修觀故。
即能出生九想。八念。十	即能出生九想。八念。十
想。八背舍。八胜处。十	想。八背捨。八勝處。十
一切处。九次第定。师子	一切處。九次第定。師子
奋迅三昧。超越三昧。练	奮迅三昧。超越三昧。練
禅。十四变化心。三明。	禪。十四變化心。三明。
六通。及八解脱。得灭受	六通。及八解脫。得滅受
想。即入涅盘。观为妙	想。即入涅槃。觀為妙
门。意在此也。五者还为	門。意在此也。五者還為
妙门者。行者若用惠行。	妙門者。行者若用惠行。
善巧破折。反本还源。是	善巧破折。反本還源。是
时即便出生空	時即便出生空

First, there is the samādhi of the wheel of earth. This is just the "preliminary ground" (*anāgamya*).

Second, there is the samādhi of the wheel of water. This is just the bringing forth of roots of goodness associated with the various types of dhyāna absorptions.

Third, there is the samādhi of the wheel of empty space. This is just where [any of] five classes of "provisional-teaching" practitioners may awaken to [dharmas based in] causes and conditions as devoid of any inherent nature and as comparable to empty space.[3]

Fourth, there is the gold-dust (lit. "gold-sand") samādhi. This is just the liberation from both view and thought [delusions]. One comes to possess herein right wisdom[4] devoid of any attachment and analogous in character to gold dust.

Fifth, there is the vajra-wheel samādhi. This is just the ninth station on the irresistible path (*ānantāryamārga*). It is able to cut off the fetters of the three realms so that they are eternally put to an end and leave no residue. **[549c]** One realizes here the knowledge of destruction (*kṣaya-jñāna*), realizes the knowledge of non-production (*anutpāda-jñāna*), and enters nirvāṇa.

As for the ability of "stabilization" to serve as a gate to the sublime, the conceptual basis for it abides in this.

D. Contemplation

Fourth, "contemplation" (*upalakṣaṇā*) as a gate to the sublime: On account of cultivating contemplation, the practitioner is then able to bring forth the nine reflections, the eight recollections, the ten reflections, the eight liberations, the eight bases of ascendancy (*abhibhvāyatana*), the ten universal bases (*kṛtsnāyatana*), the nine sequential absorptions, the lion-sport samādhi, the "over-leaping" samādhi, the "practice" dhyānas, the fourteen transformational minds, the three clarities, the six superknowledges, and also the eight liberations (sic).[5] One achieves the cessation of feeling and perception and then enters nirvāṇa. As for the ability of "contemplation" to serve as a gate to the sublime, the conceptual basis for it abides in this.

E. Turning

Fifth, "turning" (*vivartanā*) as a gate to the sublime:[6] In a case where the practitioner employs wisdom in his practice, he engages in a skillful reductive analysis whereby he turns back to the root and returns to the source. At this time he generates emptiness,

无想无作。三十七品四谛。十二因缘。中道正观。因此得入涅盘。还为妙门。意在此也。六者净为妙门者。行者若能体识一切诸法本性清净。即便获得自性禅也。得此禅故。二乘之人。定证涅盘。若是菩萨。入铁轮位。具十信心。修行不止。即便出生九种大禅。所谓自性禅。一切禅。难禅。一切门禅。善人禅。一切行禅。除恼禅。此世他世乐禅。清净禅。菩萨依是禅故。得大菩提果。已得今得当得。净为妙门。意在此也	無想無作。三十七品四諦。十二因緣。中道正觀。因此得入涅槃。還為妙門。意在此也。六者淨為妙門者。行者若能體識一切諸法本性清淨。即便獲得自性禪也。得此禪故。二乘之人。定證涅槃。若是菩薩。入鐵輪位。具十信心。修行不止。即便出生九種大禪。所謂自性禪。一切禪。難禪。一切門禪。善人禪。一切行禪。除惱禪。此世他世樂禪。清淨禪。菩薩依是禪故。得大菩提果。已得今得當得。淨為妙門。意在此也
简体字	正體字

signlessness,[7] and wishlessness, the thirty-seven wings, the four truths, the twelve causes and conditions, and the correct contemplation characteristic of the Middle Way. On account of this, he succeeds in gaining entry into nirvāṇa. As for the ability of "turning" to serve as a gate to the sublime, the conceptual basis for it abides in this.

F. Purification

Sixth, "purification" (*pariśuddhiḥ*) as a gate to the sublime: In a case where the practitioner is able to realize the fundamental purity of all dharmas, he then gains the realization of the dhyāna of [cognition of] the fundamental nature. On account of gaining this dhyāna, Two-Vehicles practitioners experience an absorption-based realization of nirvāṇa. In the case of a bodhisattva, he enters the "iron-wheel" position and embodies the mind-states inhering in the stations comprised by the ten faiths.

In a case where one continues to cultivate without stopping, he subsequently generates the nine kinds of great dhyāna, namely: the dhyāna of [cognition of] the fundamental nature, the all-encompassing dhyāna, the difficult-to-access dhyāna, the universal-gateway dhyāna, the good-person dhyāna, the dhyāna of all practices, the dhyāna which dispenses with affliction, the dhyāna of bliss in this world and other worlds, and the dhyāna of purity.

Through relying on these dhyānas, the bodhisattvas realize the fruit of the great bodhi. They have realized it before, they realize it now, and they will realize it in the future. As for the ability of "purification" to serve as a gate to the sublime, the conceptual basis for it abides in this.

[0549c19] 次释第二次第相生六妙门者。次第相生。入道之阶梯也。若于欲界中。巧行六法。第六净心成就。即发三乘无漏。况复具足诸禅三昧。此即与前有异。所以者何。如数有二种。一者修数。二者证数。修数者。行者调和气息。不澁不滑。安详徐数。从一至十。摄心在数。不令驰散。是名修数。证数者。觉心任运。从一至十。不加功力心住息缘。觉息虚微。心相渐细。患数为麁。意不欲数。尔时行者。应当放数修随。	[0549c19] 次釋第二次第相生六妙門者。次第相生。入道之階梯也。若於欲界中。巧行六法。第六淨心成就。即發三乘無漏。況復具足諸禪三昧。此即與前有異。所以者何。如數有二種。一者修數。二者證數。修數者。行者調和氣息。不澁不滑。安詳徐數。從一至十。攝心在數。不令馳散。是名修數。證數者。覺心任運。從一至十。不加功力心住息緣。覺息虛微。心相漸細。患數為麁。意不欲數。爾時行者。應當放數修隨。
简体字	正體字

Chapter Two

The Six Gates in Terms of Sequential Development

II. Six Gates Cultivation in Terms of Sequential Development

The sequential occurrence wherein each gives rise to another serves as a sequence of steps leading to one's entry into the Path. If one skillfully cultivates these six dharmas while within the desire realm, then, upon perfecting the purified mind associated with the sixth [gate], not only will one directly generate the non-outflow state common to the Three Vehicles, one will additionally succeed in perfecting all of the dhyāna samādhis.

A. Counting

This process has certain inherent differences relative to the preceding section. How is this the case? Take for example "counting." Here we distinguish two categories: The first consists in the "cultivation" of counting, whereas the second involves the "realization" of counting.

1. Cultivation

As for the cultivation of counting, the practitioner regulates and harmonizes the breath so that it is neither too rough nor too subtle. One proceeds in an unhurried fashion, slowly counting, going from "one" on up to "ten." One focuses the mind on the counting and does not allow it to run off and become scattered. This is what is meant by the "cultivation" of counting.

2. Realization

As for the realization of counting, the mind imbued with awareness exercises control from "one" on up to "ten." Without having to put forth any particular effort, the mind abides in the objective conditions associated with the breath.

When one becomes aware that the breath has become insubstantial and faint, the mind becomes gradually more subtle along with it. One subsequently becomes concerned that counting has become a coarse activity. One's state of mind is such that one does not wish to engage in counting. At just such time, the practitioner should let loose of the counting and then proceed to cultivate "following."

简体字	正體字
随亦有二。一者修随。二者证随。修随者。舍前数法。一心依随息之出入。摄心缘息。知息入出。心住息缘。无分散意。是名修随。证随者。心既微细。安静不乱。觉息长短遍身入出。心息任运相依。意虑恬然凝静。觉随为麁。心厌欲舍。如人疲极欲眠不乐众务。尔时行者。应当舍随修止。止亦有二。一者修止。二者证止。修止者。息诸缘虑。不念数随。凝寂其心。是名修止。证止者。觉身心泯然入定。	隨亦有二。一者修隨。二者證隨。修隨者。捨前數法。一心依隨息之出入。攝心緣息。知息入出。心住息緣。無分散意。是名修隨。證隨者。心既微細。安靜不亂。覺息長短遍身入出。心息任運相依。意慮恬然凝靜。覺隨為麁。心厭欲捨。如人疲極欲眠不樂眾務。爾時行者。應當捨隨修止。止亦有二。一者修止。二者證止。修止者。息諸緣慮。不念數隨。凝寂其心。是名修止。證止者。覺身心泯然入定。

B. Following

"Following" is itself of two different sorts: The first is the cultivation of following whereas the second is the realization of following.

1. Cultivation

As for the cultivation of following, one relinquishes the previous dharma of counting. One then relies single-mindedly on following the coming in and going out of the breath. One focuses the mind, taking the breath as an object. One becomes aware of the coming in and going out of the breath. **[550a]** The mind abides in the objective conditions associated with the breath, remaining free of any distraction or scattering of one's point of attention. This is what is meant by cultivating following.

2. Realization

As for the realization of following, since the mind has become fine and subtle, it becomes peaceful, still, and free of any disorderliness. One becomes aware of the breath, as now long, as now short, as now pervading the body, as now coming in, and as now going out. The mind and the breath carry on in a state of mutual interdependence. The deliberations of the mind become tranquil and fixed in a state of stillness.

Next, one becomes aware of following as a coarse activity. The mind becomes averse to it and wishes to relinquish it. This is analogous to when a person has become exhausted and desires to sleep, thus causing him to be disinclined to deal with his many tasks. At this time, the practitioner should relinquish following and then cultivate stabilization.

C. Stabilization

"Stabilization" is itself of two different sorts: The first is the cultivation of stabilization. The second is the realization of stabilization.

1. Cultivation

As for the cultivation of stabilization, one puts to rest all thought taking anything as an objective condition. One does not engage in either counting or following. One fixes his mind and makes it still. This is what is meant by the cultivation of stabilization.

2. Realization

As for the realization of stabilization, one becomes aware of the body and mind seeming to vanish entirely as he then enters into meditative absorption.

简体字	正體字
不见内外相貌。定法持	不見内外相貌。定法持
心。任运不动行者是时。	心。任運不動行者是時。
即作是念。今此三昧。虽	即作是念。今此三昧。雖
复无为寂静安隐快乐。而	復無為寂靜安隱快樂。而
无惠方便。不能破坏生	無惠方便。不能破壞生
死。复作是念。今此定	死。復作是念。今此定
者。皆属因缘阴界入法和	者。皆屬因緣陰界入法和
合而有。虚诳不实。我今	合而有。虛誑不實。我今
不见不觉。应须照了。作	不見不覺。應須照了。作
是念已。即不着止。起观	是念已。即不著止。起觀
分别。观亦有二。一者修	分別。觀亦有二。一者修
观。二者证观。修观者。	觀。二者證觀。修觀者。
于定心中。以惠分别。观	於定心中。以惠分別。觀
于微细出入息相。如空中	於微細出入息相。如空中
风。皮肉筋骨。三十六	風。皮肉筋骨。三十六
物。如芭蕉不实。心识无	物。如芭蕉不實。心識無
常。刹那不住。无有我	常。刹那不住。無有我
人。身受心法。皆无自	人。身受心法。皆無自
性。不得人法。定何所	性。不得人法。定何所
依。是名修观证观者。如	依。是名修觀證觀者。如
是观时。觉息出入遍诸毛	是觀時。覺息出入遍諸毛

One does not observe any inward or outward appearances. The dharma of absorption embraces the mind as it remains continuously unmoving. At this time, the practitioner reflects thus: "Although this samādhi is unconditioned, quiescent, secure, and blissful, nonetheless, it is devoid of any skillful means associated with wisdom. Thus it remains unable to bring about the destruction of [the cycle of] births and deaths."

One then has another thought: "This absorption belongs entirely to the sphere of causes and conditions. Its existence depends entirely on the conjunction of those causes and conditions associated with the aggregates, sense realms, and sense bases. It is false, deceptive, and not reflective of reality. I am not now exercising any perceptive acuity or any form of conscious awareness. I must bring illuminating intelligence to bear here." Having reflected thus, one then immediately becomes free of any attachment to "stabilization" and subsequently engages in the analysis associated with contemplation.

D. Contemplation

"Contemplation" is itself of two different sorts. The first is the cultivation of contemplation. The second is the realization of contemplation.

1. Cultivation

As for the cultivation of contemplation, in the midst of the mind immersed in absorption, one employs wisdom to make distinctions. One contemplates the fine and subtle features of the breath as it goes forth and comes in. It is like a wind in the midst of space. The skin, the flesh, the sinews, the bones, the thirty-six categories of things [making up the body]—are all just as devoid of substantiality as the [coreless] plantain. Even the consciousness of one's mind is impermanent. It does not abide even for a *kṣaṇa*.[1] Neither oneself nor anyone else exists. The dharmas of the body, feeling,[2] and the mind are all devoid of any inherently existent nature. One is unable to ultimately apprehend [the existence of] any person or any dharma. On what then could meditative absorption [possibly] depend? This is what is meant by the cultivation of contemplation.

2. Realization

As for the realization of contemplation, when one is contemplating in this manner, one becomes aware of the breath entering, exiting, and pervading [the entire body, extending even] to all of the hair

简体字	正體字
孔。心眼开明。彻见三十	孔。心眼開明。徹見三十
六物。及诸虫户。内外不	六物。及諸虫戶。內外不
净。刹那变易。心生悲	淨。剎那變易。心生悲
喜。得四念处。破四颠	喜。得四念處。破四顛
倒。是名证观。观相既	倒。是名證觀。觀相既
发。心缘观境。分别破	發。心緣觀境。分別破
折。觉念流动。非真实	折。覺念流動。非真實
道。尔时应当舍观修还。	道。爾時應當捨觀修還。
还亦有二。一者修还二者	還亦有二。一者修還二者
证还。修还者。既知观从	證還。修還者。既知觀從
心生。若从折境。此即不	心生。若從折境。此即不
会本源。应当反观观心。	會本源。應當反觀觀心。
此观心者。从何而生。为	此觀心者。從何而生。為
从观心生。为从非观心	從觀心生。為從非觀心
生。若从观心生。即已有	生。若從觀心生。即已有
观。今实不尔。所以者	觀。今實不爾。所以者
何。数随止等三法中。未	何。數隨止等三法中。未
有即观故。若从不观心	有即觀故。若從不觀心
生。不观心为灭生。	生。不觀心為滅生。

pores. The mind's eye opens with clarity and one thoroughly sees the thirty-six things [composing the body] as well all of the organisms therein, the inward and outward impurity, and the changes occurring even in every *kṣaṇa*. The mind becomes both saddened and delighted. One gains realization of the four stations of mindfulness and destroys the four inverted views. This is what is meant by the "realization" of contemplation.

Once the characteristic features of contemplation have developed, the mind takes the domain that is contemplated as an objective condition and proceeds then to make distinctions and deconstructing analyses with regard to it. One consequently becomes aware that [allowing] the onward-flowing movement of thought does not amount to a reality-based path. At such a time, one should then relinquish the process of contemplation and proceed instead to cultivate "turning."

E. Turning

"Turning" is itself of two different sorts. The first is the cultivation of turning. The second is the realization of turning.

1. Cultivation

As for the cultivation of turning, once one has realized that contemplation itself arises from the mind and once one has also understood that, if one continues to follow along with analysis of the objective sphere, this does not by itself directly bring about convergence with the original source, one should then turn back the direction of one's contemplation so that one now contemplates that very mind that is engaged in contemplation.

As for this mind which engages in contemplation, from what does it arise? Is it generated by contemplative thought or is it generated by something other than contemplative thought? If it is the case that it is generated by contemplative thought, then it should also be the case that there was a pre-existing contemplation process already underway. But in the present situation, this is certainly not the case. Why not? Because there was not yet anything in the midst of the three [immediately preceding] dharmas of "counting," "following," "stabilization," and so forth that was identifiable with this [process of] "contemplation."

If it is the case that [contemplative thought] arose from a mind not involved in contemplation, is it the case that the mind not involved in contemplation generated it when [that non-contemplating thought]

简体字	正體字
为不灭生。若不灭生。即	為不滅生。若不滅生。即
二心并。若灭法生灭法已	二心並。若滅法生滅法已
謝。不能生观。若言亦灭	謝。不能生觀。若言亦滅
亦不灭生。乃至非灭非不	亦不滅生。乃至非滅非不
灭生。皆不可得。当知观	滅生。皆不可得。當知觀
心本自不生。不生故不	心本自不生。不生故不
有。不有故即空。空故无	有。不有故即空。空故無
观心。若无观心。岂有观	觀心。若無觀心。豈有觀
境。境智双亡。还源之要	境。境智雙亡。還源之要
也。是名修还相。证还相	也。是名修還相。證還相
者。心惠开发。不加功	者。心惠開發。不加功
力。任运自能破折。反本	力。任運自能破折。反本
还源。是名证还。行者当	還源。是名證還。行者當
知。若离境智。欲归无境	知。若離境智。欲歸無境
智。不离境智缚。以随二	智。不離境智縛。以隨二
边故。尔时当舍还门安心	邊故。爾時當捨還門安心
净道。	淨道。

had already ceased or instead produced it when [that non-contemplating thought] had not yet ceased? If it is the case that it produced it when [that non-contemplating thought] had not ceased, then this would be a case of two thoughts existing simultaneously.

If [one were to posit that] it was generated by a dharma which had already ceased to exist, [one should realize that], once an extinct dharma has already disappeared, it is no longer able to generate any contemplative [thought process]. **[550b]**

If one were to claim that it was generated from that which had ceased and yet not ceased, or if one were to go so far as to claim that it was generated from that which had neither ceased nor not ceased, in all such cases, those [antecedent causes] cannot ultimately be apprehended. One should therefore realize that the contemplative mind itself was originally unproduced. Because it was unproduced, it does not exist. Because it does not exist, it is just "empty" [of any inherent existence]. Because it is empty [of any inherent existence], there is no mind engaged in the process of contemplation.

If there is no contemplative mind, how could there be an objective sphere which serves as the object of contemplation? This perishing of both the objective sphere and the faculty of knowing is the essential factor in turning back to the source. This is the characteristic feature of the cultivation of turning.

2. Realization

As for the characteristic feature of the realization of turning, the wisdom of the mind opens forth and develops in a way no longer requiring one to bring to bear additional skillful effort. It carries on in a way allowing one to naturally be able to invoke analyses, turn back towards the origin, and return to the source. This is what is meant by the realization of turning.

The practitioner should realize that, if he desires to retreat into [a circumstance involving] an absence of both objective sphere and knowing faculty utterly apart from an objective sphere and a knowing faculty, he would thereby fail to leave behind being tethered to [the duality inherent in] an objective sphere and a knowing faculty. This is because, in such a case, one would still simply be coursing along in the sphere of duality-based extremes. At just such a time, one should then relinquish the gateway of turning and establish the mind in the path of purification.

净亦有二。一者修净。二者证净修净者。知色净故。不起妄想分别。受想行识。亦复如是。息妄想垢。是名修净。息分别垢是名修净。息取我垢。是名修净。举要言之。若能心如本净。是名修净。亦不得能修所修及净不净。是名修净。证净者。如是修时。豁然心惠相应。无碍方便。任运开发。三昧正受。心无依恃。证净有二。一者相似证。五方便相似无漏道惠发。二者真实证。苦法忍乃至第九无碍	淨亦有二。一者修淨。二者證淨修淨者。知色淨故。不起妄想分別。受想行識。亦復如是。息妄想垢。是名修淨。息分別垢是名修淨。息取我垢。是名修淨。舉要言之。若能心如本淨。是名修淨。亦不得能修所修及淨不淨。是名修淨。證淨者。如是修時。豁然心惠相應。無礙方便。任運開發。三昧正受。心無依恃。證淨有二。一者相似證。五方便相似無漏道惠發。二者真實證。苦法忍乃至第九無礙
简体字	正體字

F. Purification

"Purification" itself is of two sorts. The first is the cultivation of purification. The second is the realization of purification.

1. Cultivation

As for the cultivation of purification, through realizing the purity of the form [aggregate], one refrains from generating false thoughts about it and does not course in discriminations regarding it. "The same is true with respect to [the aggregates of] feeling, perception, formative factors (*saṃskāras*), and consciousness."[3]

One puts to rest the defilement of false thinking. This constitutes the cultivation of purification. One also puts to rest the defilement of coursing in discriminations. This too qualifies as the cultivation of purification. One puts to rest the defilement of grasping at a self as well. This is also what is intended by "the cultivation of purification."

To state what is essential: If one is able to bring it about that his mind conforms to its fundamental purity, this qualifies as the cultivation of purification. If one does not ultimately apprehend any subjective entity which is able to cultivate, any objective sphere which is cultivated, or anything which qualifies as either "pure" or "impure," this qualifies as the cultivation of purification.

2. Realization

As for the realization of purification, when one is cultivating in this manner, one experiences a sudden penetration through to a circumstance wherein the mind accords with wisdom. Unimpeded skillful means continuously manifest and, abiding in the "direct experiencing" of samādhi,[4] the mind remains free of any dependence on anything at all.

a. Semblance Realization of Purification

This realization of purification is of two sorts: The first is a semblance of realization. This refers to the generation of a semblance of the wisdom of the non-outflow path gained through implementation of the five categories of skillful means.[5]

b. Genuine Realization of Purification

The second is genuine realization. This refers to the generation of true non-outflow wisdom as it occurs in such circumstances as the achievement of the dharma-knowledge-of-suffering patience (*duḥkhe dharmajñānakṣānti*) on up to the ninth station of the irresistible

道等真无漏惠发也。三界垢尽。故名证净。复次观众生空故名为观。观实法空故名为还。观平等空故名为净。复次空三昧相应故名为观。无相三昧相应故名为还。无作三昧相应故名为净。复次一切外观名为观。一切内观名为还。一切非内非外观名为净。故先尼梵志言。非内观故。得是智惠。非外观故。得是智惠。非内外观故。得是智惠。亦不无观故。得是智惠也	道等真無漏惠發也。三界垢盡。故名證淨。復次觀衆生空故名為觀。觀實法空故名為還。觀平等空故名為淨。復次空三昧相應故名為觀。無相三昧相應故名為還。無作三昧相應故名為淨。復次一切外觀名為觀。一切內觀名為還。一切非內非外觀名為淨。故先尼梵志言。非內觀故。得是智惠。非外觀故。得是智惠。非內外觀故。得是智惠。亦不無觀故。得是智惠也
简体字	正體字

path (*ānantāryamārga*). [Under these circumstances], the defilement characteristic of the three realms is brought to an end. Hence this is referred to as the "realization" of purification.

G. Alternative Categorizations

Then again, [one might also explain that] it is on the basis of contemplating the emptiness of beings that one defines "contemplation," that it is on the basis of contemplating the emptiness of dharmas associated with reality that one defines "turning," and that it is on the basis of contemplating uniform emptiness that one defines "purification."

Then again, [one might also explain that] it is correspondence with the samādhi of emptiness which defines "contemplation," that it is correspondence with the samādhi of signlessness that defines "turning," and that it is correspondence with the samādhi of wishlessness which defines "purification."

Then again, [one might also explain that] all outwardly-directed contemplations qualify as "contemplation," that all inwardly-directed contemplations qualify as "turning," and that all contemplations which are neither inwardly nor outwardly directed qualify as "purification." Hence Śreṇika, the Brahmacārin, stated, "It is not by virtue of an inwardly-directed contemplation that one gains this wisdom. It is not by virtue of an outwardly-directed contemplation that one gains this wisdom. It is not by virtue of a contemplation which is both inwardly-directed and outwardly-directed that one gains this wisdom. Nor is it the case that one gains this wisdom in the absence of any contemplation whatsoever."

简体字	正體字
[0550b26] 次释第三随便宜六妙门。夫行者欲得深禅定智慧。乃至实相涅盘。初学安心。必须善巧。云何善巧。当于六妙门法。悉知悉觉。调伏其心。随心所便。可以常用。所以者何。若心不便修治即无益。是故初坐时。当识调心。学数次当学随。复当学心观还等。各各经数日。学已复更从数随。乃至还净。安心修习。复各经数日。如是数反。行者即应自知心所便宜。若心便数。当以数法	**[0550b26]** 次釋第三隨便宜六妙門。夫行者欲得深禪定智慧。乃至實相涅槃。初學安心。必須善巧。云何善巧。當於六妙門法。悉知悉覺。調伏其心。隨心所便。可以常用。所以者何。若心不便修治即無益。是故初坐時。當識調心。學數次當學隨。復當學心觀還等。各各經數日。學已復更從數隨。乃至還淨。安心修習。復各經數日。如是數反。行者即應自知心所便宜。若心便數。當以數法

Chapter Three

The Six Gates in Accordance with Suitability

III. Six Gates Cultivation in Accordance with Suitability

A. On the Need for Skillfulness

Now the practitioner wishes to gain the realization of deep dhyāna absorption and wisdom which extend all the way to the true character of phenomena and to nirvāṇa. Thus, as one who is at the initial stage of study strives to stabilize the mind, he must be proficient in his skillfulness. How is it that he is proficient in skillfulness? It should be that, with respect to the dharmas of the six gates to the sublime, one is entirely knowledgeable and entirely aware.

B. General Principles

In the training and subduing of one's own mind, one may employ in constant use whatsoever serves to facilitate [the training of] the mind. Why is this? If the mind is not well-facilitated [by the methods employed], then the process of cultivation and correction will remain ineffective. Therefore, when one first engages in sitting [meditation], one should recognize [the correct method for] regulating the mind. **[550c]**

1. On the Correct Process

After having trained in "counting," one should next train in "following." Additionally, one should move along to the study of "stabilization,"[1] "contemplation," "turning," and so forth. In each endeavor, one should spend several days.

Having completed this course of training, one should once again proceed with an additional course whereby one starts with "counting" and "following" and proceeds on along through to "turning" and "purification," establishing the mind in this manner of cultivation and practice by once again spending several days with each separate endeavor. One should proceed in this manner through several complete courses.

a. On Realizing what is Actually Suitable

The practitioner should then naturally know what the mind finds to be suitable. If the mind finds "counting" to be suitable, then one should avail oneself of the dharma of "counting" in establishing

简体字	正體字
安心。乃至净亦如是。随便而用不简次第如是安心时。若觉身安息调。心静开明。始终安固。当专用此法。必有深利。若有妨生心散暗塞。当更随便转用馀门。安即为善。可以长轨。是则略明初学善巧安心六妙门。是知便宜用心大意。复次行者。心若安稳必有所证。云何为证。所谓得持身及麁住细住。欲界未到地初禅等种种诸禅定。得诸定已。若心住不进。当随定深浅。修六妙门开发。云何名浅定不进修六门令进。如行者初得持身法。及麁	安心。乃至淨亦如是。隨便而用不簡次第如是安心時。若覺身安息調。心靜開明。始終安固。當專用此法。必有深利。若有妨生心散闇塞。當更隨便轉用餘門。安即為善。可以長軌。是則略明初學善巧安心六妙門。是知便宜用心大意。復次行者。心若安穩必有所證。云何為證。所謂得持身及麁住細住。欲界未到地初禪等種種諸禪定。得諸定已。若心住不進。當隨定深淺。修六妙門開發。云何名淺定不進修六門令進。如行者初得持身法。及麁

the mind in calmness. This would also be the case with any of the methods on up to and including "purification." One accords with what is found to be suitable and thus proceeds with using that.

b. On Ensuring That Choices Are Actually Beneficial

One should not, in any case, neglect any steps in proper sequence. As one proceeds in this manner with establishing the mind in calmness, once one has become aware that the body has become calm, that the breath has become well-regulated, that the mind has become quiescent and has developed clarity, and that, from beginning-to-end, one remains peaceful and stable, then one should primarily employ this particular method. There will certainly be profound benefit from this.

If it is the case that there is some associated problem involving the generation of scatteredness, darkness, or obstruction of the mind, then one should once again accord with what is suitable and then change to the use of one of the other gates.

It is the establishment in tranquility which qualifies as good here. One may take that as an enduring standard.

This then concludes a summary clarification of how the beginning student applies proficiency in skillfulness to establishing the mind in the six gates to the sublime. Through this, one may know the major import of employing what is suitable in applying the mind.

C. Specifics of Cultivation

1. Recognizing what Constitutes Evidence of Realization

Moreover, if the practitioner's mind remains stable, it will certainly be the case that there will be realizations. So what is it that constitutes "realization"? This refers to the gaining of the so-called "physical support" as well as "coarse abiding," "subtle abiding," the desire-realm preliminary ground (*anāgamya*), the first dhyāna, and all sorts of other dhyāna absorptions.

2. Recognizing Absence of Progress; Adopting Appropriate Strategies

Once one has already achieved the absorptions, if the mind simply abides in them and does not advance, then, according to the depth of the absorption, one should cultivate further development of the six gates to the sublime. What is meant by "when absorption is shallow and there is no advancement, one proceeds to cultivate the six gates to the sublime in order to cause advancement"?

Take for example when the practitioner first achieves the dharma of "physical support" as well as the dharmas of "coarse abiding"

细住法。经于日月而不增进。尔时应当细心修数。数若不进。复当修随。随若不进。当细凝心修止。止若不进。当定中观阴入界法。观若不进。当还更反检心源。还若不进。当寂然体净。用此六法。若偏于一法。增进之时。当即善修之。既渐进入深禅定。便过数境。数相既谢。进发随禅。于此定中。若不境进。当善修随止观还净等五法。定进渐深。随境已度。若发止禅。禅若不进。当善修止及观还净等四法。止定进渐深。观心开发。虽有止法。知从缘生无有自性。	細住法。經於日月而不增進。爾時應當細心修數。數若不進。復當修隨。隨若不進。當細凝心修止。止若不進。當定中觀陰入界法。觀若不進。當還更反檢心源。還若不進。當寂然體淨。用此六法。若偏於一法。增進之時。當即善修之。既漸進入深禪定。便過數境。數相既謝。進發隨禪。於此定中。若不境進。當善修隨止觀還淨等五法。定進漸深。隨境已度。若發止禪。禪若不進。當善修止及觀還淨等四法。止定進漸深。觀心開發。雖有止法。知從緣生無有自性。
简体字	正體字

and "subtle abiding." If one passes through days or months in this way and yet does not progress beyond this circumstance, one should then employ a subtle mind in the cultivation of "counting."

If one does not advance through "counting," then one should next cultivate "following." If one does not advance through "following," one should subtly still (lit. "freeze") the mind in the cultivation of "stabilization." If one does not advance through "stabilization," then, in the midst of absorption, one should engage in "contemplation" of the dharmas of the aggregates, the sense bases, and the sense realms.

If one does not advance through "contemplation," then one should engage in "turning," turning back yet again to investigation of the source of the mind. If one does not advance through "turning," then one should quiescently embody the realization of "purification." If, in utilizing these six dharmas, one inclines towards a single one of the dharmas, provided that it brings enhanced progression, one should immediately proceed with skillfully cultivating it.

Having gradually advanced and entered into deep dhyāna absorption, one then passes beyond the mind state associated with "counting." Once the characteristic features of [the mind state associated with] "counting" have receded, one advances into the development of dhyāna associated with "following."

However, if it happens that, when one is in this absorption, the associated mind state does not develop progressively, one should then engage in skillful cultivation of the five dharmas of following, stabilization, contemplation, turning, purification, and so forth. The absorption then advances and gradually deepens.

Once the state associated with "following" has been traversed, it will then be as if one has generated the dhyāna associated with "stabilization." However, if one's dhyāna does not progress at that point, one should then engage in skillful cultivation of the four dharmas of stabilization, contemplation, turning, purification, and so forth.

The absorption associated with stabilization then progresses and gradually deepens. The mind associated with "contemplation" then opens forth and develops.

Now, although one possesses this dharma of "stabilization," one nonetheless realizes that it is something produced solely from conditions and, as such, it is devoid of any inherently-existent nature.

止相已謝。若观禅不进。当更善巧修观及还净等三法。观禅既进。进已若謝。转入深定。惠解开发。唯觉自心所有法相。知观虚诳不实亦在妄情。如梦中所见。知已不受。还反照心源。还禅经久。又不进。当复更善反观心源。及体净当寂。还禅既进。进已若謝。便发净禅。此禅念相观已除。言语法皆灭。无量众罪除。清净心常一。是名净禅。净若不进。当善却垢心。体真寂虚。心如虚空。无所依倚。尔时净禅渐深寂。豁然明朗发	止相已謝。若觀禪不進。當更善巧修觀及還淨等三法。觀禪既進。進已若謝。轉入深定。惠解開發。唯覺自心所有法相。知觀虛誑不實亦在妄情。如夢中所見。知已不受。還反照心源。還禪經久。又不進。當復更善反觀心源。及體淨當寂。還禪既進。進已若謝。便發淨禪。此禪念相觀已除。言語法皆滅。無量眾罪除。清淨心常一。是名淨禪。淨若不進。當善却垢心。體真寂虛。心如虛空。無所依倚。爾時淨禪漸深寂。豁然明朗發
简体字	正體字

Once the characteristic features of "stabilization" have already receded, if the dhyāna associated with "contemplation" does not progress, then one should engage in yet more skillful cultivation of the three dharmas of contemplation, turning, purification, and so forth.

Once this contemplation-based dhyāna has progressed, even having already progressed, it may seem then as if it has receded. It then transforms in a way that one enters into deep meditative absorption. At that point, one's wise understanding develops. One then abides in a state wherein one is aware only of all of the dharmic characteristics of his own mind.

One should then realize that this "contemplation" itself is false, deceptive, and unreal and that it, too, belongs to the sphere of false mental impressions. It is comparable to one's perceptions while in a dream state. Once one has realized this, one no longer simply accepts it.[2] One instead engages in "turning" through which one reverses the direction of one's focus to illuminate the very source of the mind itself. **[551a]**

After the dhyāna associated with "turning" has persisted for a long while, if one once again finds that there is no further progression, one should apply even greater skillfulness in turning around one's contemplations to focus on the very source of one's mind, even to the point where one embodies a realization of the purity of that stillness one has encountered.

Once this turning-based dhyāna has progressed—even having already progressed, it may seem as if it has receded. One then proceeds to manifest the dhyāna associated with "purification." In this dhyāna, "conceptual contemplations have already been gotten rid of and the dharmas of words and speech have already perished. The immeasurable multitude of offenses are gotten rid of and the purified mind remains eternally unified."[3] This is what is meant by the dhyāna of "purification."

If, however, one does not experience a progression of "purification," one should bring particular skillfulness to one's banishment of the defiled mind. One comes to embody a realization of the quiescence and emptiness of genuine reality. One's mind becomes like empty space and has nothing whatsoever upon which it relies.

At this time, one's purification-based dhyāna becomes gradually ever more deep and quiescent. Then, suddenly, and as if breaking through, there manifests brilliant clarity and the generation of the

真无漏。证三乘道。此则略说六妙门。随便宜而用增长诸禅功德智惠。乃至入涅盘也。复次行者。于其中间。若有内外障起。欲除却者。亦当于六门中。随取一法。一一试用却之。若得差者即为药也。治禅障及禅中魔事病患。功用六门悉得差也。上来所说。其意难见。行者若用此法门。当善思推取意。勿妄行也	真無漏。證三乘道。此則略說六妙門。隨便宜而用增長諸禪功德智惠。乃至入涅槃也。復次行者。於其中間。若有內外障起。欲除却者。亦當於六門中。隨取一法。一一試用却之。若得差者即為藥也。治禪障及禪中魔事病患。功用六門悉得差也。上來所說。其意難見。行者若用此法門。當善思推取意。勿妄行也
简体字	正體字

genuine state of being "beyond outflow-impurities." One thereby achieves realization of the path of the Three Vehicles.

D. Summary Statement on Suitability

This then is a summary discussion of the six gates to the sublime wherein one utilizes whatsoever is suitable, increases the merit and wisdom associated with the dhyānas, and then finally gains entry into nirvāṇa.

Additionally, if the practitioner encounters the arising of inward or outward obstacles during the midst of this and so desires to get rid of them, in this case as well, he should select a corresponding method from among the six gates. He should try each one of the gates, one after the other, utilizing them to get rid of such obstacles. If, through employing a given method, he brings about a cure, then that very measure constitutes precisely the appropriate medicine.

In countering dhyāna-related obstacles as well as demon-linked phenomena and pathological disorders occurring in dhyāna, resorting to skillful use of the six gates will succeed in bringing about a cure in every case.

One may find it difficult to perceive the meaning implicit in the preceding discussion. If the practitioner utilizes these gateways to Dharma, he should deduce their import by engaging in skillful deliberative reflection upon them. One must not simply practice them in an error-ridden manner.

[0551a14] 次释第四对治六妙门。三乘行者。修道会真。悉是除障显理。无所造作。所以者何。二乘之人。四住惑除。名得圣果。更无别法。菩萨大士。破尘沙无明障尽故。菩提理显。亦不异修。此而惟之。若能巧用六门对治。破内外障。即是修道。即是得道更无别道。云何功用六门对治。行者应当知病识药。云何知病。所谓三障。一者报障。即是今世不善。麁动散乱障界入也。	[0551a14] 次釋第四對治六妙門。三乘行者。修道會真。悉是除障顯理。無所造作。所以者何。二乘之人。四住惑除。名得聖果。更無別法。菩薩大士。破塵沙無明障盡故。菩提理顯。亦不異修。此而惟之。若能巧用六門對治。破內外障。即是修道。即是得道更無別道。云何功用六門對治。行者應當知病識藥。云何知病。所謂三障。一者報障。即是今世不善。麁動散亂障界入也。
简体字	正體字

Chapter Four

The Six Gates as Means of Counteraction

IV. Six Gates Cultivation as Means of Counteraction

A. General Clarification: Cultivation Consists Primarily of Remediation

As the practitioner of the Three Vehicles cultivates the Path and converges with the truth, in every case, this is an exercise in getting rid of obstacles and manifesting the noumenal [reality].[1] There is nothing whatsoever which is being "created" in this endeavor. How is this the case?

For Two-Vehicles practitioners,[2] once they have gotten rid of the delusions corresponding to the four dwelling stations (*āvāsa-bhūmi*),[3] this qualifies as realization of "the fruit of [the path of] the Ārya."[4] They do not have any additional dharma above and beyond that.

Because the great bodhisattva eminences utterly destroy the obstacle of "dust-and-sand" delusions, they manifest the noumenal [reality] of bodhi. They, too, do not cultivate anything aside from this.

Thus one may realize through extrapolation that, if one is merely able to skillfully employ the six gates as countermeasures in the destruction of inward and outward obstacles, it is just this very activity which constitutes cultivation of the Path. It is just this very thing which constitutes realization of the Path. There is no other "Path" aside from this.

B. Specific Countermeasures: Addressing the Three Obstacles

How is it that one puts these six gates to effective use as countermeasures? The practitioner should recognize the appropriate medicine based on a knowledge of the particular disease. How does one know the nature of the disease? It is just the so-called "three obstacles" (*āvaraṇa*).

The first are the "retribution-related obstacles" (*vipāka-āvaraṇa*). They are just the unfortunate occurrences of this very life and the scatteredness and confusion associated with coarse agitation. They constitute obstacles with respect to the sense realms and the sense bases.

简体字	正體字
二者烦恼障。即三毒十使等诸烦恼也。三者业障。即是过去现在所起障道恶业。于未受报中间。能障圣道也。行者于坐禅中。此三障发。当善识其相。用此法门。对治除灭。云何坐中知报障起相。云何对治等。分别觉观心。散动攀缘诸境无暂停住。故名报障起。浮动明利。攀缘诸境。心散纵横。如猿猴得树。难可制录尔时行者应用数门。调心数息当知即真对治也。故佛言。觉观多者。教令数息。二者于坐禅中。或时其心亦昏亦散。昏即无记心。暗即睡眠。散即心浮越逸。尔时行者。当用随门。善调	二者煩惱障。即三毒十使等諸煩惱也。三者業障。即是過去現在所起障道惡業。於未受報中間。能障聖道也。行者於坐禪中。此三障發。當善識其相。用此法門。對治除滅。云何坐中知報障起相。云何對治等。分別覺觀心。散動攀緣諸境無暫停住。故名報障起。浮動明利。攀緣諸境。心散縱橫。如猿猴得樹。難可制錄爾時行者應用數門。調心數息當知即真對治也。故佛言。覺觀多者。教令數息。二者於坐禪中。或時其心亦昏亦散。昏即無記心。闇即睡眠。散即心浮越逸。爾時行者。當用隨門。善調

The second are the "affliction-related obstacles" (*kleśa-āvaraṇa*). They are just all such afflictions as are associated with the three poisons,[5] the ten agents,[6] and so forth.

The third are the "karma-related obstacles" (*karma-āvaraṇa*). They are just [the effects of] the bad karma obstructing the path which has arisen from past and present [causes]. During that period when one has still not undergone the associated retribution, they are able to obstruct [realization of] the path of the Āryas.

When the practitioner is sitting in dhyāna meditation, if these three obstacles manifest, he should skillfully recognize their characteristics and use these Dharma gates to counteract and get rid of them. How is it that, as one is sitting, one is aware of the characteristics of the arising of retribution-related obstacles, and how is it that one should engage in such endeavors as are involved in counteracting them?

1. Counteracting Retribution-Related Obstacles: Specific Strategies

a. "Counting" to Counteract Uncontrolled Ideation

When discrimination-making initial ideation (*vitarka*) and mental discursion (*vicāra*)[7] manifest ceaseless scattered movement and manipulation of the objective sphere—it is then that we speak of the arising of retribution-related obstacles.

When the mental floating and moving about is obvious and acute, and when it is engaged in manipulations of the objective sphere—when the mind scatters vertically and laterally like a monkey in a tree—when this is so extreme that it is difficult to control or keep track of it—it is then that the practitioner should employ the gate of "counting," thus training the mind to count the breaths. One should realize that, in such a situation, it is precisely this which qualifies as the genuinely counteractive technique. [551b] Hence the Buddha stated that, for those in whom primary ideation and mental discursion are abundant, one should teach them to count the breaths.

b. "Following" to Counteract Dullness, Scatteredness, and Drowsiness

Second, when one is sitting in dhyāna meditation, there may be times when one's mind is both dull and scattered. "Dullness" is marked by the non-recalling mind. "Dimness," [which may be an associated factor], is marked by drowsiness. "Scatteredness" is marked by the "floating," "skipping-over," and "running off" of one's thoughts.

When these circumstances present themselves, the practitioner should employ the gate of "following," skillfully training the

简体字	正體字
心随息。明照入出。心依息缘。无分散意。照息出入。治无记昏睡心。依于息治觉观攀缘三者于坐禅中。若觉身心急气麁心散流动尔时行者。当用止门。宽身放息。制心凝寂。止诸忆虑。此为治也。复次云何烦恼障起。云何对治。烦恼有三种。一者于坐禅中。贪欲烦恼障起。尔时行者。当用观心门中九想。初背舍。二胜处。诸不净门。为对治也。二者于坐禅中。瞋恚烦恼障起。尔时行者。当用观心门中慈悲喜舍等。为对治也。	心隨息。明照入出。心依息緣。無分散意。照息出入。治無記昏睡心。依於息治覺觀攀緣三者於坐禪中。若覺身心急氣麁心散流動爾時行者。當用止門。寬身放息。制心凝寂。止諸憶慮。此為治也。復次云何煩惱障起。云何對治。煩惱有三種。一者於坐禪中。貪欲煩惱障起。爾時行者。當用觀心門中九想。初背捨。二勝處。諸不淨門。為對治也。二者於坐禪中。瞋恚煩惱障起。爾時行者。當用觀心門中慈悲喜捨等。為對治也。

mind to follow the breath as one clearly illuminates the entering and exiting of one's respiration. The mind thus comes to abide in dependence upon the breath as an objective condition [and it follows that] there is no further division or scattering of the mental attention. As [the mind] "illuminates" the going out and coming in of the breath, this counters mind states involving non-recall, dullness, and drowsiness. As it abides in dependence upon the breath, one counters the mind's primary ideation, mental discursion, and manipulation of the objective sphere.

c. Stabilization to Counteract Urgency, Coarseness, and Rumination

Third, if while one is sitting in dhyāna meditation, one becomes aware of an urgency in body and mind manifesting as coarseness of the breath together with a scatteredness and continuous flowing on of thought, the practitioner should then employ the gate of "stabilization" to relax the body, "release" the breath, and control the thought so that it becomes focused in stillness. One thus brings all recollection and rumination to a halt. This is the appropriate counteractive technique in such cases.

2. Counteracting Affliction-related Obstacles: Specific Strategies

Next, how is it that affliction-related obstacles are generated and how is it that one should counteract them? Afflictions (*kleśa*) are of three primary types:

a. Desire

In the case of the first, when one is sitting in dhyāna meditation, it may be that the affliction of desire arises. At such a time, the practitioner should resort to the gate of "contemplation of mind," employing the nine reflections on the unlovely,[8] the initial contemplations involved in the [eight] liberations,[9] the [first] two of the [eight] bases of ascendancy,[10] and any other of the methods for realization of "impurity."[11] These are the appropriate counteractive techniques in such circumstances.

b. Hatred

In the case of the second, when one is sitting in dhyāna meditation, it may be that the affliction of hatred arises. At such a time, the practitioner should resort to the gate of "contemplation of mind," engaging in the contemplations of loving-kindness, compassion, sympathetic joy, equanimity, and so forth. These are the appropriate counteractive techniques in such circumstances.

三者于坐禅中。愚痴邪见烦恼障起。尔时行者。当用还门。反照十二因缘三空道品破折心源还归本性。此为治也。复次云何对治障道业起业即三种。治法亦三。一者于坐禅中。忽然垢心昏暗。迷失境界。当知黑暗业障起尔时行者。当用净门中念方便净应身三十二相清净光明。为对治也。二者于坐禅中。忽然恶念。思惟贪欲。无恶不造。当亦是过去罪业所之作也。尔时行者。当用净门中念报佛一切种智	三者於坐禪中。愚癡邪見煩惱障起。爾時行者。當用還門。反照十二因緣三空道品破折心源還歸本性。此為治也。復次云何對治障道業起業即三種。治法亦三。一者於坐禪中。忽然垢心昏闇。迷失境界。當知黑闇業障起爾時行者。當用淨門中念方便淨應身三十二相清淨光明。為對治也。二者於坐禪中。忽然惡念。思惟貪欲。無惡不造。當亦是過去罪業所之作也。爾時行者。當用淨門中念報佛一切種智
简体字	正體字

c. Delusive Ignorance

In the case of the third, when one is sitting in dhyāna, it may be that the affliction of delusion arises along with its erroneous views. At such a time, the practitioner should employ the gate of "turning," turning back his attention to illuminate the twelve causes and conditions, the three emptinesses,[12] and the [thirty-seven] wings of enlightenment, engaging in analysis directed at the very source of his own mind, and returning in refuge to its fundamental nature. This is the appropriate counteractive technique to for use in such circumstances.

3. Counteracting Karmic Obstacles: Specific Strategies

Then again, just how is it that one goes about counteracting the karma obstructing the Path? Karma arises in three ways. The means for counteracting it are also threefold:

a. Counteracting Defiled Thought Involving Mental Turbidity

In the case of the first, when one is sitting in dhyāna meditation, it may be that there suddenly arise defiled thoughts accompanied by mental turbidity, dimness, and the loss through such confusion of one's meditative mind state. One should then realize that this is a circumstance involving the arising of obstacles originating from one's previous black and murky karmic actions.

At such a time, the practitioner should resort to an approach associated with the gate of "purification," specifically using as a counteractive technique mindfulness of the pure light issuing from the thirty-two marks of [a buddha's] transformation body (*nirmāṇa-kāya*) wherein "purity associated with the provisional"[13] manifests. This is the appropriate counteractive technique in such circumstances.

b. Counteracting Desire-Related Defiled Thought

In the case of the second, when one is sitting in dhyāna meditation, it may be that there suddenly arise unwholesome thoughts wherein one deliberates on ideas associated with sensual desire and wherein there is no unwholesome karma which one would not commit. It is likely in this case as well that this is a circumstance generated by the karma of past transgressions.

At such a time, the practitioner should resort to an approach associated with the gate of "purification," specifically using as a counteractive technique mindfulness of a reward-body (*saṃbhogha-kāya*) buddha's qualities of: the knowledge of all modes (*sarva-ākāra-jñatā*),

简体字	正體字
圆净常乐功德。为对治	圓淨常樂功德。為對治
也。三者于坐禅中。若有	也。三者於坐禪中。若有
种种诸恶境界相现。乃至	種種諸惡境界相現。乃至
逼迫身心。当知悉是过去	逼迫身心。當知悉是過去
今世所造恶业障发也。尔	今世所造惡業障發也。爾
时行者。当用净门中念法	時行者。當用淨門中念法
身本净不生不灭本性清	身本淨不生不滅本性清
净。为对治也。此则略说	淨。為對治也。此則略說
六门对治断除三障之相。	六門對治斷除三障之相。
广说不异。十五种障也。	廣說不異。十五種障也。
复次行者。于坐禅中。若	復次行者。於坐禪中。若
发诸馀禅深定智惠解脱。	發諸餘禪深定智惠解脫。
有种种障起。当于六门	有種種障起。當於六門
中。善巧用对治法也。麁	中。善巧用對治法也。麁
细障法既除。真如实相自	細障法既除。真如實相自
显。三明六通自发。十力	顯。三明六通自發。十力
四无所畏。一切诸佛菩萨	四無所畏。一切諸佛菩薩
功德行愿。自然现前不由	功德行願。自然現前不由
造作。故经云。又见诸如	造作。故經云。又見諸如
来自然成佛道	來自然成佛道

"perfect purity,"[14] permanence, and bliss. This is the appropriate counteractive technique in such circumstances.

c. Counteracting Abhorrent Mind States

In the case of the third, when one is sitting in dhyāna meditation, signs may appear which are linked to all manner of abhorrent states of mind which, in the extreme case, may even involve [visions of] subjection to physical and mental coercion. One should realize that such signs are all a product of obstacles generated by unwholesome karmic actions committed in past and present lives.

At such a time, the practitioner should resort to an approach associated with the gate of "purification," specifically using as a counteractive technique mindfulness of the Dharma-body (*dharma-kāya*) [buddha's] "fundamental purity,"[15] [focusing] on its being neither-produced-nor-destroyed and on its possessing a fundamental nature characterized by purity. This is the appropriate counteractive technique in such circumstances.

C. General Summation

This has been a general explanation of the aspects involved in employing the six gates as counteractive methods to cut off and eliminate the three obstacles. An extensive explanation would not differ from a treatment of the fifteen kinds of obstacles.[16]

1. Regarding Sudden Arising of Obstacles

Additionally, suppose that the practitioner has been sitting in dhyāna meditation in a circumstance wherein there have already manifested all other sorts of deep dhyāna absorptions, wisdom, and liberations, but then all sorts of obstacles arise. In such a case, one should then skillfully select and employ the appropriate counteractive techniques from among the six gates.

2. Benefits of Correct Implementation

Once both the coarse and subtle obstructive dharmas have already been eliminated the true suchness and the true character of phenomena will then naturally manifest. [551c] The three clarities (*vidyā*)[17] and the six superknowledges (*abhijña*) will be spontaneously generated. The ten powers, four fearlessnesses, meritorious qualities, practices, and vows of all buddhas and bodhisattvas will all naturally appear before one. All of these phenomena will come into being without any deliberate effort being made to cause their manifestation. Hence the *Sutra* states, "I see as well all of the Tathāgatas naturally realizing the path of buddhahood."[18]

[0551c05] 次释第五相摄六妙门。夫六妙门相摄。近论则有二种。远寻则有多途。何等为二。一者六门自体相摄。二者巧修六门。出生胜进相摄。云何名自体相摄。行者修六门时。于一数息中。任运自摄随止观还净等五法。所以者何。如行者善调心数息之时。即体是数门。心依随息而数故。即摄随门。息诸攀缘。制心在数故。即摄心门。分别知心数法及息。了了分明故。即摄观门。若心动散。攀缘五欲。悉是虚诳。心不受着缘心还归	**[0551c05]** 次釋第五相攝六妙門。夫六妙門相攝。近論則有二種。遠尋則有多途。何等為二。一者六門自體相攝。二者巧修六門。出生勝進相攝。云何名自體相攝。行者修六門時。於一數息中。任運自攝隨止觀還淨等五法。所以者何。如行者善調心數息之時。即體是數門。心依隨息而數故。即攝隨門。息諸攀緣。制心在數故。即攝心門。分別知心數法及息。了了分明故。即攝觀門。若心動散。攀緣五欲。悉是虛誑。心不受著緣心還歸
简体字	正體字

Chapter Five

The Six Gates in Terms of Mutual Inclusion

V. Six Gates Cultivation in Terms of Mutual Inclusion

Now, as for the mutual inclusiveness of the six gates to the sublime, to speak of it in near terms, there are two categories. When the concept is carried further, this involves many pathways. Precisely what are the two types?

As for the first of these categories, it is the mutual inclusiveness of the very substance of the six gates. In the case of the second, it is that mutual inclusiveness whereby skillful cultivation of the six gates generates superior progress.

A. Mutual Inclusiveness of the Very Substance

So what precisely is meant by "mutual inclusiveness of the very substance"? When the practitioner is cultivating the six gates, during the course of his "counting" of a single breath he is carrying on as well an inherent inclusion of the other five dharmas of following, stabilization, contemplation, turning, and purification.

How is this the case? Take for instance when the practitioner is skillfully training the mind to count the breaths. The very substance [of that practice] is the gate of "counting." Because the mind depends upon following the breath to perform the practice of counting, that very practice also includes the gate of "following." Because one puts to rest all grasping at [extraneous] objective conditions and controls the mind so that it abides in the practice of counting, that very practice includes the gate of "stabilization."[1]

Because one is engaged in the process of distinguishing and remaining aware of both that dharma of mental counting and also the [character of the] breath, doing so in a manner characterized by complete clarity, that very practice includes the gate of contemplation as well.

In a case where the mind moves and becomes scattered as it proceeds to grasp at objects of the five types of desire, [one subsequently realizes that] all such phenomena are false and deceptive. The mind then no longer acquiesces in attachment to those objective conditions. Because the mind then "turns back," returning

简体字	正體字
数息故。即摄还门。摄数息时。无有五盖及诸麁烦恼垢身心寂然。即摄净门。当知于数息中。即有六门。随止观还净等。一一皆摄六门此则六六三十六妙门。上来虽复种种运用不同悉有今意。若不分别。行人不知。此则略说六妙门。自体相摄一中具六相也。复次云何名巧修六妙门出生胜进相摄相。行者于初。调心数息。从一至十。心不分散。是名数门。当数息时。静心善巧。既知息初入中间经游至处。乃至入已还出亦如是心悉觉知。依随不乱。亦成就数法。从一至十。是则数中成就随门。复次行者。当数息时。细心	數息故。即攝還門。攝數息時。無有五蓋及諸麁煩惱垢身心寂然。即攝淨門。當知於數息中。即有六門。隨止觀還淨等。一一皆攝六門此則六六三十六妙門。上來雖復種種運用不同悉有今意。若不分別。行人不知。此則略說六妙門。自體相攝一中具六相也。復次云何名巧修六妙門出生勝進相攝相。行者於初。調心數息。從一至十。心不分散。是名數門。當數息時。靜心善巧。既知息初入中間經遊至處。乃至入已還出亦如是心悉覺知。依隨不亂。亦成就數法。從一至十。是則數中成就隨門。復次行者。當數息時。細心

again to the counting of the breaths, that [very practice of counting] includes the gate of "turning" as well.

When one is engaged in focusing on the counting of the breaths, one remains free of the five hindrances (*nīvaraṇa*) or any of the defilements associated with the coarse afflictions. Both the body and mind then come to abide in a state of quiescence. Thus that [very practice of counting] is itself also inclusive of the gate of "purification."

One should realize that within that very practice of counting the breaths, there exist [all of] the six gates. Each and every one of the practices of following, stabilization, contemplation, turning, and purification is inclusive of the six gates. This being the case, there are then six times six, that is to say thirty-six gates to the sublime.

In the case of the topics previously taken up, although their particular implementations differ, still, they all embody the present concept. If we failed to make these distinctions, the practitioner would remain unaware of them. This then is a brief explanation of how the six gates to the sublime, in their very substance, are so mutually inclusive that all six characteristics are embodied within each one of them.

B. Mutual Inclusiveness Where Skillfulness Generates Superior Progress

Next, what are the characteristic features of that mutual inclusiveness whereby skillful cultivation of the six gates to the sublime generates superior progress?

At the beginning, when the practitioner is training the mind to count the breaths from "one" up to "ten" such that the mind does not split off and become scattered, this constitutes the gate of "counting." Precisely when one is engaged in this practice of counting, the quiescent mind is engaged in a skillful way. Having remained aware of the breath's initial entry, its internal route of travel, and the location to which it reaches, this continues on as, even after the breath has entered, the mind remains entirely aware as it goes back on out again.

It is through relying on "following," that one remains undistracted and thus becomes able to accomplish the perfection of the dharma of "counting," going from "one" on up to "ten." In doing this, even while engaged in the practice of "counting," one achieves the perfection of the gate of "following."

Additionally, at precisely that time when the practitioner is engaged in the counting of the breaths, the subtle mind is engaged

简体字	正體字
善巧。制心缘数法及息。不令细微觉观得起刹那异念分别不生。是则于数中。成就止门。复次行者。当数息时。成就息念巧惠方便。用静鉴之心。照息生灭。兼知身分刹那思想。阴入界法如云如影。空无自性。不得人法。是时于数息中。成就息念巧惠观门。复次行者。当数息时。非但成就观智。识前法虚假。亦复善巧觉了观照之心。无有自性虚诳不实。离知觉想。是则于数息中。成就还门。复次行者。当数息时。非但不得所观能观以惠方便。亦不得无能观所观。以本净法性如虚空。不可分别故。	善巧。制心緣數法及息。不令細微覺觀得起剎那異念分別不生。是則於數中。成就止門。復次行者。當數息時。成就息念巧惠方便。用靜鑒之心。照息生滅。兼知身分剎那思想。陰入界法如雲如影。空無自性。不得人法。是時於數息中。成就息念巧惠觀門。復次行者。當數息時。非但成就觀智。識前法虛假。亦復善巧覺了觀照之心。無有自性虛誑不實。離知覺想。是則於數息中。成就還門。復次行者。當數息時。非但不得所觀能觀以惠方便。亦不得無能觀所觀。以本淨法性如虛空。不可分別故。

in a skillful manner. It controls the mind so that it takes as its object the practice of "counting" as well as the breath itself. It does not allow either subtle primary ideation (*vitarka*) or mental discursion (*vicāra*) to succeed in arising. Thus not even a *kṣaṇa* of variant thought or discrimination is permitted to arise. This being the case, one is then able, even while engaged in "counting," to accomplish the perfection of the gate of "stabilization."

Additionally, at just that time that the practitioner is engaged in counting the breaths, he perfects the skillful means of discerning wisdom (*saṃprajñāna*)[2] in mindfulness of the breath. He utilizes the mind of quiescent reflection to illuminate the arising and cessation of the breath. He simultaneously becomes aware of the constituents of his body even at the *kṣaṇa*-after-*kṣaṇa* [micro-moment] level of thought. He becomes aware that the aggregates, sense bases, and sense realms are all just like clouds and just like shadows, while also realizing that they are empty and devoid of any inherently existent nature of their own. **[552a]**

Thus [the practitioner] finds he is unable to apprehend [any objective evidence of] either a "person" or a "dharma." At this time, even while engaged in the practice of counting the breaths, he perfects the gate of "contemplation" through employing discerning wisdom to his mindfulness of the breath.

Moreover, at just that time when the practitioner is engaged in counting the breaths, it is not that he only accomplishes that perfection of contemplative wisdom which recognizes presently manifest dharmas as false. Rather, utilizing excellent skillfulness, he also becomes entirely aware that this very mind engaged in contemplative illumination is itself devoid of any inherently existent nature and is false, deceptive, and unreal. He then abandons thought devoted to carrying on knowing awareness [of the objective sphere]. In doing this, even while engaged in counting the breaths, he perfects the gate of "turning."

Additionally, at just that time when the practitioner is engaged in counting the breaths, it is not that he merely fails to apprehend any objective sphere which is contemplated or any subjective agent which is able to contemplate. Additionally, by employing wisdom-based skillful means, he is also unable to conclude that contemplator and contemplated are [definitively] non-existent either. This is because the fundamentally pure nature of dharmas is like empty space and cannot be made the object of discriminating analysis.

尔时行者。心同法性。寂然不动。是则于数息中。成就净门。以五门庄严数息。随止观还净。皆亦如是。今不别说。此则六六三十六。亦名三十六妙门。行者若能如是善巧修习六妙门者。当知必得种种诸深禅定智惠。入三乘涅盘也	爾時行者。心同法性。寂然不動。是則於數息中。成就淨門。以五門莊嚴數息。隨止觀還淨。皆亦如是。今不別說。此則六六三十六。亦名三十六妙門。行者若能如是善巧修習六妙門者。當知必得種種諸深禪定智惠。入三乘涅槃也
简体字	正體字

At this time, the mind of the practitioner is [realized to be] identical to the very nature of dharmas. It is quiescent and does not move. In this then, even while engaged in counting the breaths, one perfects the gate of "purification."

C. General Summation

One thus employs the other five gates as adornments to the practice of counting the breaths. In every case, "following," "stabilization," "contemplation," "turning," and "purification" are all also just like this. However, we shall not now take up those separate discussions. In this case then, there are six times six, or thirty-six permutations which may be collectively referred to as "the thirty-six gates to the sublime."

One should realize that, if the practitioner is able to employ excellent skillfulness in the cultivation and practice of the six gates to the sublime, he will certainly succeed in realizing many types of deep dhyāna absorption and wisdom and will enter into that nirvāṇa which is common to all Three Vehicles.

[0552a14] 次释第六通别六妙门。所以言通别六门者。凡夫外道二乘菩萨通观数息一法。而解惠不同。是故证涅盘殊别。随止观还净亦复如是所以者何。凡夫钝根行者。当数息时唯知从一至十。令心安定。欲望此入禅受诸快乐。是名于数息中而起魔业。以贪生死故。复次如诸利根外道见心猛盛见因缘故。当数息时非但调心数息。从一至十。欲求禅定。亦能分别现在有息无息。亦有亦无。非有非无。过去息如去不如去。亦如去亦不如去。	[0552a14] 次釋第六通別六妙門。所以言通別六門者。凡夫外道二乘菩薩通觀數息一法。而解惠不同。是故證涅槃殊別。隨止觀還淨亦復如是所以者何。凡夫鈍根行者。當數息時唯知從一至十。令心安定。欲望此入禪受諸快樂。是名於數息中而起魔業。以貪生死故。復次如諸利根外道見心猛盛見因緣故。當數息時非但調心數息。從一至十。欲求禪定。亦能分別現在有息無息。亦有亦無。非有非無。過去息如去不如去。亦如去亦不如去。
简体字	正體字

Chapter Six

The Six Gates in Terms of Identities and Differences

VI. Six Gates Cultivation in Accordance with Identities and Differences

A. The Rationale Behind This Analytic Discussion

As for the reason for speaking of the six gates to the sublime according to identities and differences, common people, non-Buddhists, Two-Vehicles practitioners, and bodhisattvas each generally do contemplate the one single dharma of "counting" of the breath. However, the wisdom through which they understand matters is not identical. They are therefore distinctly different as regards the issue of realization of nirvāṇa. This is also the case as regards the practices of "following, "stabilization," "contemplation," "turning," and "purification." How is this the case?

B. Specific Cases

1. Deviant Practitioners

When a practitioner who is a common person of dull faculties takes up the practice of counting the breaths, he knows only to go from "one" on up to "ten" in order to cause the mind to become stabilized. He looks to this out of a desire to enter dhyāna and experience all manner of pleasurable effects from it. Because this amounts to covetousness in pursuit of [desirable aspects of] cyclic existence, it constitutes the generation of demon karma from within the practice of counting the breaths.

2. Non-Buddhists

Then again, take for example those non-Buddhists of sharp faculties whose "view-associated" thought is fierce and abundant. On account of the causes and conditions associated with "views," precisely when they are engaged in the practice of counting the breaths, they are not only training the mind to count the breaths, going from "one" on up to "ten," desiring to thereby achieve dhyāna stabilization. They are also able to engage in discriminations whereby they determine with respect to the present moment whether the breath exists or does not exist, whether it is both existent and non-existent, or whether it is neither existent nor non-existent.

They determine with respect to past breaths whether they are past or are not past, whether they are both past and yet not past,

简体字	正體字
非如去非不如去。未来息有边无边。亦有边亦无边。非有边非无边。现在息有常耶无常耶。亦常亦无常耶。非常非无常耶。及心亦尔。随心所见。计以为实。谓他所说。悉为忘语。是人不了息相。随妄见生分别。即是数息戏论。四边火烧。生烦恼处。长夜贪着邪见。造诸邪行。断灭善根。不曾无生。心行理外。故名外道。如是二人钝利虽殊。三界生死轮迴无别。复次云何名为声闻数息相。行者欲速出三界。自求涅盘故。修数息以调其心尔时于数息中。不离四谛正观。云何于数息中。观四真谛。行者知息依身身依心。三事和合	非如去非不如去。未來息有邊無邊。亦有邊亦無邊。非有邊非無邊。現在息有常耶無常耶。亦常亦無常耶。非常非無常耶。及心亦爾。隨心所見。計以為實。謂他所說。悉為忘語。是人不了息相。隨妄見生分別。即是數息戲論。四邊火燒。生煩惱處。長夜貪著邪見。造諸邪行。斷滅善根。不曾無生。心行理外。故名外道。如是二人鈍利雖殊。三界生死輪迴無別。復次云何名為聲聞數息相。行者欲速出三界。自求涅槃故。修數息以調其心爾時於數息中。不離四諦正觀。云何於數息中。觀四真諦。行者知息依身身依心。三事和合

and whether they are neither past nor not past. They determine with respect to future breaths whether they are limited or limitless, whether they are both limited and limitless, and whether they are neither limited nor limitless. They determine whether the breaths in the present are permanent or whether they are impermanent, whether they are both permanent and impermanent, and whether they are neither permanent nor impermanent.

This [obsession with their own views] also extends to the sphere of "thought" in the same way. Thus, whatsoever their mind succeeds in perceiving is therefore deemed by them to be genuine. They are of the opinion that whatsoever is claimed by others is all false discourse. These persons do not completely understand the characteristics of the breath. They follow along with false views and generate discriminations accordingly.

This just amounts to frivolous discourse concerned with the counting of the breaths. It is a case of being burned by the fire of the *tetralemma* and is an arena for the generation of afflictions. During the long night [of time], such individuals remain covetously attached to erroneous views and engage in all manner of erroneous actions. They cut off and destroy their roots of goodness and fail to encounter the unproduced.[1] [552b] It is because their minds course outside of the sphere of the noumenal reality that they are referred to as "outside" traditions (*tīrthika*).

3. Commonalities Between Deviant Practitioners and Non-Buddhists

Although people of the above two types differ as regards dullness and sharpness of faculties, there really is no practical distinction as regards [their both being trapped in] the cycle of birth and death within the three realms.

4. The Śrāvakas' Use of Breath Meditation in Cultivating the Truths

Next, what are the characteristic features of the Śrāvaka Disciples' counting of the breaths? Because the practitioner desires to depart rapidly from the three realms and thus engages in a personal quest for nirvāṇa, he cultivates the counting of the breaths in order to train his mind. At that time, while he is engaged in the practice of counting of the breaths, he does not depart from an orthodox contemplation of the four truths. How is it that, even when engaged in counting the breaths, he contemplates the four truths?

a. The Truth of Suffering

The practitioner knows that the breath depends upon the body and that the body depends upon the mind. Taken together, these three

简体字	正體字
名阴界入。阴界入者即是苦也。若人贪着阴界入法。乃至随逐见心。分别阴界入法。即名为集。若能达息真性。即能知苦无生。不起四受。四行不生即钝使利使。诸烦恼结。寂然不起。故名为灭。知苦正惠。能通理无壅。故名为道。若能如是数息。通达四谛当知是人必定得声闻道。毕故不造新。复次云何于数息中。入缘觉道行者求自然惠。乐独善寂。深知诸法因缘。当数	名陰界入。陰界入者即是苦也。若人貪著陰界入法。乃至隨逐見心。分別陰界入法。即名為集。若能達息真性。即能知苦無生。不起四受。四行不生即鈍使利使。諸煩惱結。寂然不起。故名為滅。知苦正惠。能通理無壅。故名為道。若能如是數息。通達四諦當知是人必定得聲聞道。畢故不造新。復次云何於數息中。入緣覺道行者求自然惠。樂獨善寂。深知諸法因緣。當數

phenomena are referred to as the [five] aggregates, the sense realms, and the sense bases. The aggregates, sense realms, and sense bases are themselves synonymous with suffering.

b. The Truth of Accumulation

If a person becomes covetously attached to the dharmas of the aggregates, sense realms, and sense bases or goes so far as to pursue view-ridden thoughts devoted to making discriminations among dharmas of the aggregates, sense realms, and sense bases, it is precisely that which serves as the basis of "accumulation."

c. The Truth of Cessation

If one is able to penetrate through to an understanding of the true nature of the breath, then one is able to realize suffering itself is unproduced. Thus the four classes of feeling[2] do not arise. Since [categorical bases of] the four practice-aspects [of the truth of suffering][3] are [realized as] not produced, then the dull agents,[4] the sharp agents,[5] and all of the affliction-related fetters (*saṃyojana*) remain quiescent and do not arise. Thus it is that we refer to "cessation."

d. The Truth of the Path

That right wisdom which knows [the truth of] suffering is able to penetrate through to the noumenal reality without any obstruction. Thus it is that we refer to "the Path."

e. Summation on Śrāvaka Disciple Practice

If there is someone who is able in this fashion to practice counting of the breaths and who is thus able to gain a penetrative understanding of the four truths—one should be aware that this individual will most definitely achieve realization of the path of the Śrāvaka Disciples. Then, having reached its end, he does not engage in the creation of anything new beyond that.[6]

5. The Pratyekabuddhas

Next, how is it that, while engaged in the practice of counting the breaths, one enters the path of those "awakened through conditions" (*pratyekabuddha*)?

a. The Pratyekabuddha's Breath-Based Twelve-Links Meditation

[In such a case], the practitioner seeks sovereignly initiated wisdom, takes pleasure in solitude, esteems stillness, and becomes profoundly aware of the causes and conditions associated with dharmas. At precisely the time in which he is engaged in the counting of

简体字	正體字
息时。即知数息之念即是	息時。即知數息之念即是
有支。有缘取。取缘爱爱	有支。有緣取。取緣愛愛
缘受。受缘触。触缘六	緣受。受緣觸。觸緣六
入。六入缘名色。名色缘	入。六入緣名色。名色緣
识。识缘行。行缘无明。	識。識緣行。行緣無明。
复观此息念之有。名善有	復觀此息念之有。名善有
为业。有善因缘。必定能	為業。有善因緣。必定能
感未来世人天受。受因缘	感未來世人天受。受因緣
故。必有老死忧悲苦恼。	故。必有老死憂悲苦惱。
三世因缘。生死无际。轮	三世因緣。生死無際。輪
转不息。本无有生。亦无	轉不息。本無有生。亦無
有死。不善思惟心行所	有死。不善思惟心行所
造。若知无明体性本自不	造。若知無明體性本自不
有。妄想因缘和合而生。	有。妄想因緣和合而生。
无所有故。假名无明。无	無所有故。假名無明。無
明尚尔。亦不可得。当知	明尚爾。亦不可得。當知
行等诸因缘法。皆无根	行等諸因緣法。皆無根
本。既无行等因缘。岂有	本。既無行等因緣。豈有
今之数息之实。尔时行	今之數息之實。爾時行
者。深知数	者。深知數

the breaths, he concurrently knows that this very thought which is engaged in counting the breaths is just the "becoming" component [of the twelve-fold chain of causality].

[He realizes that] "becoming" is conditioned by "grasping," that "grasping" is conditioned by "craving," that "craving" is conditioned by "feeling," that "feeling" is conditioned by "contact," that "contact" is conditioned by "the six sense bases," that "the six sense bases" are conditioned by "name-and-form," that "name-and-form" is conditioned by "consciousness," that "consciousness" is conditioned by "karmic formative factors" (*saṃskāra,*) and that such "formative factors" are conditioned by "ignorance."

He continues to contemplate the "becoming" constituted by this breath-associated thought. It is identified as wholesome conditioned karmic activity possessed of wholesome causes and conditions definitely capable of bringing forth "feeling" during future human and celestial rebirths. [He realizes that], because it constitutes a cause and a condition for "feeling," it will definitely entail the existence of aging, death, worry, lamentation, and suffering-laden afflictions.

[He realizes that] the causes and conditions of the three periods of time involve boundless coursing in births and deaths continuing on in a ceaseless cycle. [He also realizes that] there is fundamentally no birth whatsoever nor is there any death whatsoever. They are [realized to be] simply a creation of mental activity arising from unwholesome thought.

If he realizes that, at root, the essential nature of "ignorance" itself is nonexistent and that it is produced through a conjunction of causes and conditions associated with erroneous perception, then [he will also realize that], because it has no [inherent] existence at all, it is only referred to as "ignorance" on the basis of false names.

[He then realizes that], if this is the case even for [the link of] "ignorance"—if not even it can be gotten at— then one should realize as well that "karmic action" and all of the other dharmas [making up the chain of] causes and conditions are in every case devoid of any fundamental basis. Since [he realizes that] there is no [intrinsic] existence on the part of "karmic activity" or any of the other causes and conditions, [he then wonders], "How could there be any reality to this present counting of the breaths?"

b. The Consequences of the Pratyekabuddha's Cultivation

At this time, [having carried out the preceding contemplation], the practitioner experiences a profound realization that the counting

息属因缘空无自性。不受不着。不念不分别。心如虚空。寂然不动。豁然无漏心生成缘觉道。复次云何名为菩萨数息相。行者为求一切智佛智自然智无师智。如来知见力无所畏。愍念安乐无量众生故修数息。欲因此法门入一切种智。所以者何。如经中说阿那般那。三世诸佛入道之初门。是故新发心菩萨欲求佛道应先调心数息。当数息时。知息非息犹如幻化。是故息非是生死。亦非是涅盘。尔时于数息中。不得生死可断。不得涅盘可入。是故不住生死。既无二十五有系缚。不证涅盘。则不堕声闻辟支佛地。	息屬因緣空無自性。不受不著。不念不分別。心如虛空。寂然不動。豁然無漏心生成緣覺道。復次云何名為菩薩數息相。行者為求一切智佛智自然智無師智。如來知見力無所畏。愍念安樂無量眾生故修數息。欲因此法門入一切種智。所以者何。如經中說阿那般那。三世諸佛入道之初門。是故新發心菩薩欲求佛道應先調心數息。當數息時。知息非息猶如幻化。是故息非是生死。亦非是涅槃。爾時於數息中。不得生死可斷。不得涅槃可入。是故不住生死。既無二十五有繫縛。不證涅槃。則不墮聲聞辟支佛地。
简体字	正體字

of the breaths belongs to the sphere of causes and conditions and that it is empty and devoid of any inherently existent nature of its own. Thus he does not take it on or become attached to it. He does not hold it in his thought and does not engage in making discriminations with regard to it. His mind becomes like empty space, quiescent, and unmoving. Then, suddenly and expansively, the mind free of outflow-impurities is generated and he thereby achieves realization of the path of those who are awakened through [the contemplation of] conditions.

6. The Bodhisattvas

Then again, what are the characteristic features of the bodhisattva's counting of the breaths? It is on account of seeking all-knowledge (*sarvajñatā*), the wisdom of the Buddha, spontaneous wisdom, the wisdom arising without reliance on a teacher, and the knowledge, vision, powers, and fearlessnesses of the Tathāgatas, that the practitioner abides in compassionate mindfulness bent on establishing innumerable beings in happiness.

a. The Bodhisattva's Breath-Based Meditation

Based on this, he proceeds with cultivating the counting of the breaths. [552c] He wishes, on account of this Dharma entryway, to enter the knowledge of all modes (*sarva-ākāra-jñatā*). Why is this? As stated in the scriptures, *ānāpāna* (meditation on the breath) is the initial gateway for entry into the path which has been utilized by all buddhas of three periods of time. Therefore, the bodhisattva who has newly brought forth the [bodhi] resolve and who wishes to seek the path of buddhahood should first train his mind in the counting of the breaths.

b. The Consequences of the Bodhisattva's Breath-Based Cultivation

At just that time when one is engaged in the counting of the breaths, he realizes that the breath is non-breath and is like a magical conjuration. [He realizes] therefore that it is not the case that the breath is [solely in the sphere of] birth-and-death nor is it the case that it is [solely in the domain of] nirvāṇa.

At that very time, in the midst of the breath, he is unable to apprehend a birth-and-death which might be cut off. Nor does he apprehend a nirvāṇa into which one might enter. Hence he does not abide [any longer] in birth-and death. Since he has become free of the bondage of the twenty-five stations of existence, he does not opt for the realization of nirvāṇa and so does not fall down onto the grounds of the Śrāvaka Disciples and the Pratyekabuddhas.

简体字	正體字
以平等大惠。即无取舍心。入息中道。名见佛性得无生忍。住大涅盘常乐我净。故经云。譬如大水能突荡一切。唯除杨柳。以其软故。生死大水。亦复如是。能漂没一切凡夫之人。唯除菩萨住于大乘大般涅盘。心柔软故。是名大乘行者。于数息中入菩萨位。此则略说数息妙门凡圣大小乘通别之相。数息虽通。须解殊别之相。当知数息虽同共修。随其果报差降。馀随止观还净一一妙门。凡圣大小乘通别。亦复如是	以平等大惠。即無取捨心。入息中道。名見佛性得無生忍。住大涅槃常樂我淨。故經云。譬如大水能突蕩一切。唯除楊柳。以其軟故。生死大水。亦復如是。能漂沒一切凡夫之人。唯除菩薩住於大乘大般涅槃。心柔軟故。是名大乘行者。於數息中入菩薩位。此則略說數息妙門凡聖大小乘通別之相。數息雖通。須解殊別之相。當知數息雖同共修。隨其果報差降。餘隨止觀還淨一一妙門。凡聖大小乘通別。亦復如是

Employing the uniform great wisdom—this is just the mind which is free of both grasping and rejecting—he enters the Middle Way [through meditation on] the breath. This refers to perceiving the nature of buddhahood, realizing the unproduced-dharmas patience, and abiding in the permanence, bliss, self, and purity of nirvāṇa.

Thus it is that the *Sutra* states, "This is analogous to the great flood which is able to inundate and wash away everything with the sole exception of the willow which remains on account of its flexibility. The great flood of birth-and-death is just the same in this regard. It is able to submerge and drown all common persons with the sole exception of the bodhisattva who abides in the great *parinirvāṇa* of the Great Vehicle. This is on account of the pliancy of his mind."[7]

It is these factors which characterize the practitioner of the Great Vehicle who, even in the midst of the counting of the breaths, gains entry into the bodhisattva position (*bodhisattvaniyāma*).[8]

C. Summation of the Identities and Differences Discussion

This then has been a brief explanation of the characteristic features marking the points of identity and difference between the common person and the ārya, and between the Great Vehicle and the Small Vehicle. Although the factor of counting the breaths is common to all of them, it is necessary to understand the characteristics which distinguish them.

One should also realize that, although counting the breaths is a shared practice cultivated by all [of these practitioners], still, each category corresponds to a different grade of resultant retribution. In just this same way, there are points of identity and difference among common persons, the Āryas, the Great Vehicle, and the Small Vehicle as regards each and every one of the other gates to the sublime: following, stabilization, contemplation, turning, and purification.

简体字	正體字
[0552c19] 次释第七旋转六妙门。上来所说六妙门。悉是共行。与凡夫二乘共故。今此旋转六妙门者。唯独菩萨所行。不与声闻缘觉共。况诸凡夫。所以者何。前第六通别妙门观中说。名从假入空观。得惠眼一切智。慧眼一切智。是二乘菩萨共法。今明从空出假旋转六妙门。即是法眼道种智。法眼道种智。不与声闻辟支佛共。云何菩萨。于数息道中。修从空出假观。起旋转出一切诸行功德	[0552c19] 次釋第七旋轉六妙門。上來所說六妙門。悉是共行。與凡夫二乘共故。今此旋轉六妙門者。唯獨菩薩所行。不與聲聞緣覺共。況諸凡夫。所以者何。前第六通別妙門觀中說。名從假入空觀。得惠眼一切智。慧眼一切智。是二乘菩薩共法。今明從空出假旋轉六妙門。即是法眼道種智。法眼道種智。不與聲聞辟支佛共。云何菩薩。於數息道中。修從空出假觀。起旋轉出一切諸行功德

Chapter Seven

The Six Gates in Accordance with Reversed Orientation

VII. Six Gates Cultivation in Accordance with Reverse-Oriented Practice

A. The Exclusive Nature of this Practice

In the case of the previously-described [modes of cultivating] the six gates to the sublime, they are all "common-practice" approaches. This is because they are [potentially] held in common with common persons and Two-Vehicles practitioners. Now, as for this cultivation of the six gates to the sublime carried out in the "reversed" orientation, it is such as is practiced by the bodhisattvas alone. It is not a practice held in common even with the Śrāvaka Disciples or the Pratyekabuddhas, how much the less with common people.

How is this the case? In the case of the immediately preceding sixth chapter, "the six gates to the sublime according to identities and differences," in the discussion of that contemplation, it was with reference to going from the contemplation of the conventional into the contemplation of emptiness. It involved gaining comprehensive-knowledge (*sarvajñatā*) as perceived with the wisdom eye. "Comprehensive knowledge as perceived with the wisdom eye" is a dharma held in common by Two-Vehicles practitioners and bodhisattvas.

Now, however, we are explaining cultivation of the six gates to the sublime carried out in the "reversed" orientation which involves emerging from the contemplation of emptiness into the contemplation of the conventional. This is just the knowledge of all modes (*sarva-ākāra-jñatā*) as perceived with the Dharma eye. The knowledge of all modes as perceived with the Dharma eye is not shared in common with the Śrāvaka Disciples and the Pratyekabuddhas.

B. Specifics of this Exclusively-Bodhisattvic Practice

1. This Practice in Relation to Mindfulness of the Breath

How is it that the bodhisattva, even while engaged in the path of counting the breaths, cultivates emerging from the contemplation of emptiness into the contemplation of the conventional, brings forth the "reversed" orientation, and generates the meritorious-quality characteristics of all of the [bodhisattva] practices?[1]

简体字	正體字
相。所谓菩萨行者。当数息时。当发大誓愿怜愍众生虽知众生毕竟空。而欲成就众生净佛国土。尽未来际。作是愿已。即当了所数息不生不灭。其性空寂。即息是空。非息灭空。息性自空。息即是空。空即是息。离空无息。离息无空。一切诸法。亦复如是。息空故非真非假。非世间非出世间。求息不得息与非息。而亦成就息念其所成就息念。如梦如幻。如响如化虽无实事可得。而亦分别幻化所作事。菩萨了息。亦复如是。虽无息性可得。而亦成就息念。从一至十。了了分明。深心分别如幻息相。	相。所謂菩薩行者。當數息時。當發大誓願怜愍眾生雖知眾生畢竟空。而欲成就眾生淨佛國土。盡未來際。作是願已。即當了所數息不生不滅。其性空寂。即息是空。非息滅空。息性自空。息即是空。空即是息。離空無息。離息無空。一切諸法。亦復如是。息空故非真非假。非世間非出世間。求息不得息與非息。而亦成就息念其所成就息念。如夢如幻。如響如化雖無實事可得。而亦分別幻化所作事。菩薩了息。亦復如是。雖無息性可得。而亦成就息念。從一至十。了了分明。深心分別如幻息相。

a. The Paradox of Emptiness and Generation of the Bodhisattva Vow

As for what is referred to as "the bodhisattva practice," even at that very time in which one is engaged in the counting of the breaths, one should generate the great vow and abide in compassionate regard for beings. Even though one realizes that beings are ultimately empty of inherent existence, still, one wishes to bring beings to perfection and purify the buddhalands, carrying on with this practice to the very exhaustion of future time. **[553a]**

b. The Identification of the Breath with Emptiness

After one has made this vow, one should immediately and completely understand that those very breaths which are being counted are not produced and not destroyed. Their nature is emptiness and quiescence. Whatsoever is breath is just emptiness.

This is not a case of emptiness arrived at in the aftermath of the breath's destruction. Rather, it is that the very nature of the breath is that it is inherently empty. The very breath itself is identical to emptiness. The very emptiness itself is identical with the breath. Apart from the emptiness, there is no breath. Apart from the breath, there is no emptiness. This is the case with all other dharmas in precisely the same way.

c. The Realization of the Illusory Nature of the Breath

Because the breath is empty of inherent existence, it is neither genuine nor false. It is neither worldly nor supramundane. One seeks to find the breath, is unable to apprehend either breath or non-breath, and yet still is able to perfect the mindfulness of the breath. That mindfulness of the breath which one perfects is like a dream, like an illusory conjuration, like an echo, and like a [supernatural] transformation. Although there is no genuine phenomenon which can be apprehended, still one engages in the making of distinctions with regard to the phenomena created through conjuration and [supernatural] transformation.

The bodhisattva's complete understanding of the breath is just like this. Although there is no [inherently-existent] nature of the breath which can be discovered, still, he perfects the mindfulness of the breath as he proceeds from "one" on up to "ten," with complete and utter distinctness and clarity. With profound depth of mind, he distinguishes the characteristics of that very breath which, in nature, is like a mere conjuration.

简体字	正體字
以有无性如幻息故。即有无性世间出世间法。所以者何。无明颠倒。不知息性空故。妄计有息。即生人法执着爱见诸行。故名世间。因有息故。即有阴界入等世间苦乐之果。当知息虽空。亦能成办一切世间善恶因果。二十五有诸生死事。复次息相空中虽无出世间相。而非不因息分别出世间法。所以者何。不知息相空故。即无明不了。造世间业。知息空无所有故。即无无明妄执一切诸结烦恼。无所从生。是名出世间因。因灭故。得离后世世间二十五有等果。名出世间果。能	以有無性如幻息故。即有無性世間出世間法。所以者何。無明顛倒。不知息性空故。妄計有息。即生人法執著愛見諸行。故名世間。因有息故。即有陰界入等世間苦樂之果。當知息雖空。亦能成辦一切世間善惡因果。二十五有諸生死事。復次息相空中雖無出世間相。而非不因息分別出世間法。所以者何。不知息相空故。即無明不了。造世間業。知息空無所有故。即無無明妄執一切諸結煩惱。無所從生。是名出世間因。因滅故。得離後世世間二十五有等果。名出世間果。能

简体字 正體字

d. Breath-Based Practice in Relation to Causality

1) The Role of Breath in Compelling Cyclic Existence

It is on account of the existence of the breath, itself devoid of any [inherently-existent] nature and like a mere conjuration, that there come to exist the worldly and supramundane dharmas which are themselves devoid of any [inherently-existent] nature. How is this the case? It is on account of the inverted views associated with delusive ignorance (*avidyā*) and the failure to realize that the nature of the breath is emptiness, that one falsely reckons that the breath actually exists.

One consequently generates attachment to persons and dharmas and engages in practices rooted in affection and views. It is on account of this that we have what one refers to as "the world." It is on account of [reckoning] that the breath exists that one then comes to have the aggregates, the sense realms, the sense bases, and the other resultant effects associated with undergoing worldly suffering and happiness.

One should realize that, although the breath is empty, it is still able to bring about the accomplishment of every form of cause-and-effect within the sphere of worldly good and evil as well as the phenomena of birth and death within the twenty-five stations of existence.

2) The Role of Breath in Conquest of the Supramundane

Additionally, although no signs of the supramundane exist in that emptiness characterizing the breath's features, it is still not the case that one does not use the breath as a causal basis in distinguishing supramundane dharmas.

How is this so? It is on account of failing to realize that the characteristic features of the breath are empty that one becomes deluded, fails to abide in complete understanding, and thus then engages in the creation of worldly karmic deeds. It is on account of realizing that the breath is empty and devoid of anything whatsoever that one consequently becomes free of delusion and the false attachment to all forms of fetters and afflictions. [One realizes that] there is no basis for their arising. This [realization] constitutes a causal basis for transcending the world.

It is on account of the cessation of their causes that one succeeds in separating from the twenty-five stations of existence and other such subsequent-lifetime resultant effects. It is this which qualifies as the supramundane resultant effect. When one is able to go

简体字	正體字
出世间颠倒因果法故。是名出世间法。于出世间真正法中。亦有因果。因者知息空。正智惠为出世间因。妄计息中人。我无明颠倒。及苦果灭故。名为出世间果。故知菩萨观息非息。虽不得世间出世间。亦能分别世间及出世间。复次菩萨。观息性空时不得四谛。而亦通达四谛。所以者何。如上所说世间果者。即是苦谛。世间因者。即是集谛。出世间果者。即是灭谛。出世间因者。即是道谛故观于息想。不见四谛。而能了了分别四谛。为声闻众生。广演分别。复次菩萨。了息空中。不见十二因缘。而亦通达十二因缘。所以者何。过去息性空无所有。	出世間顛倒因果法故。是名出世間法。於出世間真正法中。亦有因果。因者知息空。正智惠為出世間因。妄計息中人。我無明顛倒。及苦果滅故。名為出世間果。故知菩薩觀息非息。雖不得世間出世間。亦能分別世間及出世間。復次菩薩。觀息性空時不得四諦。而亦通達四諦。所以者何。如上所說世間果者。即是苦諦。世間因者。即是集諦。出世間果者。即是滅諦。出世間因者。即是道諦故觀於息想。不見四諦。而能了了分別四諦。為聲聞眾生。廣演分別。復次菩薩。了息空中。不見十二因緣。而亦通達十二因緣。所以者何。過去息性空無所有。

beyond the cause-and-effect dharmas linked to the world's inverted views, it is this which qualifies as supramundane Dharma.

Cause-and-effect still exists within the domain of the supramundane genuine right Dharma. As for the cause, it is the awareness of the emptiness of the breath as realized by right wisdom which constitutes the supramundane cause. It is the cessation of the false reckoning of the existence of persons and a self, the cessation of delusion and inverted views, and also the cessation of resultant effects characterized by suffering which [collectively] constitute the supramundane resultant effects.

Thus one realizes that the bodhisattva contemplates the breath as non-breath. Although he is unable to apprehend [any dharma which ultimately qualifies as] either "worldly" or "supramundane," still, he is able to make distinctions with regard to both the worldly and the supramundane.

e. Breath-Based Practice in Relation to the Four Truths

Additionally, when the bodhisattva contemplates the nature of the breath as empty, he does not apprehend the four truths, and yet he still penetratingly understands the four truths. How is this the case?

Worldly resultant effects such as described above are identical with the truth of suffering. Causes of that which is worldly are identical with the truth of accumulation. Supramundane resultant effects are identical with the truth of cessation. The causes for the transcendence of the world are identical with the truth of the Path.

Thus the thought utilized in the contemplation of the breath does not perceive [the ultimately real existence of] the four truths and yet is able to utterly and completely make distinctions with regard to the four truths. [553b] Thus it is that, for the sake of those beings who are śrāvaka-path practitioners, he broadly proclaims such distinctions.

f. Breath-Based Practice in Relation to the Twelve-Fold Causality

Additionally, the bodhisattva, even in the midst of his complete understanding of the emptiness of the breath, does not engender any perception of [the ultimate existence of] the twelve causes and conditions. Still, he penetratingly understands the twelve causes and conditions.

How is this the case? [The bodhisattva realizes that] the nature of past breaths is emptiness and the absence of any existent entity. [He

简体字	正體字
妄见有息。而生种种颠倒分别。起诸烦恼。故名无明。无明因缘。则有行识名色六入触受爱取有生老死忧悲苦恼等。轮转不息。皆由不了息如虚空无所有故。若知息空寂。即破无明。无明灭故。则十二因缘皆灭。菩萨如是了息非息。虽不得十二因缘。亦能了了。通达十二因缘。为求缘觉乘人。广演分别。复次菩萨了息无性。尔时尚不见有息。何况于息道中。见有六蔽及六度法。虽于息性中不见蔽及六度法。而亦了了通达六蔽六度。所以者何。行者当数息时。即自了知。若于非息之中	妄見有息。而生種種顛倒分別。起諸煩惱。故名無明。無明因緣。則有行識名色六入觸受愛取有生老死憂悲苦惱等。輪轉不息。皆由不了息如虛空無所有故。若知息空寂。即破無明。無明滅故。則十二因緣皆滅。菩薩如是了息非息。雖不得十二因緣。亦能了了。通達十二因緣。為求緣覺乘人。廣演分別。復次菩薩了息無性。爾時尚不見有息。何況於息道中。見有六蔽及六度法。雖於息性中不見蔽及六度法。而亦了了通達六蔽六度。所以者何。行者當數息時。即自了知。若於非息之中

realizes that it is because] one has falsely perceived the existence of the breath that one has thus generated all manner of inverted views and discriminations and brought forth all manner of afflictions. Thus it is that we refer to this as "delusive ignorance."[2]

Where one has ignorance serving as a cause and a condition, one consequently has karmic formative factors (*saṃskāra*), consciousness, name-and-form, the six sense bases, contact, sensation, craving, grasping, becoming, birth, aging, sickness, and death, along with misery, lamentation, suffering, affliction, and so forth. This continues on in an unceasing cycle. All of these factors arise on account of not completely understanding that the breath is like empty space and is devoid of any [inherently] existent entity whatsoever.

If one realizes that the breath is empty and quiescent, then one smashes ignorance. Because one destroys ignorance, then the twelve causes and conditions are all consequently entirely destroyed.

In this fashion, the bodhisattva completely understands the breath as non-breath and, although he does not apprehend [any ultimate existence of] the twelve causes and conditions, he is still able to completely and utterly understand them. Possessing a penetrating understanding of the twelve causes and conditions, he then broadly proclaims distinctions regarding them for the sake of practitioners seeking to realize the Pratyekabuddha-Vehicle path.

g. Breath-Based Practice in Relation to the Six Perfections

1) Breath's Transcendent Nature in Relation to the Perfections

Additionally, the bodhisattva completely understands that the breath is devoid of any [inherently existent] nature. At this time, he does not perceive even any existence of the breath, how much the less does he perceive within the pathways of the breath either the dharmas of the six obstructive conditions[3] (*ṣaḍ-vipakṣa*) or the dharmas of the six perfections.

a) Breath-Based Practice in Relation to the Perfection of Giving

i) The Role of the Breath in Engendering Covetousness

Although he does not perceive in the nature of the breath either the obstructive conditions or the dharmas of the six perfections, still, he possesses a complete and utterly penetrative understanding of the six obstructive conditions and the six perfections. How is this the case? At that very time when the practitioner is engaged in the counting of the breaths, he immediately and naturally understands completely that if, in the midst of that which is non-breath,

而见息者。是必定成就悭贪蔽法。悭有四种。一者悭惜财物。见息中有我。为我生悭故。二者悭身。于息中起身见故。三者悭命。于息中不了计有命故。四者恼法于息中不了。即起见执法心生故行者为破坏如是悭蔽恶法故。修四种檀波罗密。一者知息空非我。离息亦无我。既不得我。聚诸财物。何所资给。尔时悭财之心。即便之心。即便自息。舍诸珍宝。如弃涕唾当知了达息性。即是财施檀波罗蜜。复次菩萨。知无身性。息等诸法。不名为身。离	而見息者。是必定成就慳貪蔽法。慳有四種。一者慳惜財物。見息中有我。為我生慳故。二者慳身。於息中起身見故。三者慳命。於息中不了計有命故。四者惱法於息中不了。即起見執法心生故行者為破壞如是慳蔽惡法故。修四種檀波羅密。一者知息空非我。離息亦無我。既不得我。聚諸財物。何所資給。爾時慳財之心。即便之心。即便自息。捨諸珍寶。如棄涕唾當知了達息性。即是財施檀波羅蜜。復次菩薩。知無身性。息等諸法。不名為身。離
简体字	正體字

he nonetheless perceives the [inherent existence of] breath, this will definitely lead to the establishment of the obstructing dharmas of covetousness.

ii) The Four Types of Covetousness

There are four categories of covetousness:

The first is covetous cherishing of material forms of wealth. One perceives the existence of a self in the midst of the breath. It is for the sake of the self that one then generates covetousness.

The second is covetousness with respect to the body. This arises because one generates the view of a physical body in the midst of the breath.

The third is covetousness with respect to a lifespan. This arises because, in the midst of the breath, one fails to abide in complete understanding and so reckons that there exists a lifespan.

The fourth is covetousness with respect to the Dharma.[4] This develops because, in the midst of the breath, one fails to abide in complete understanding. One then generates views. Consequently there then arise thoughts attached to Dharma.

iii) Four Classes of Perfection of Giving

In order to demolish the evil dharmas associated with the obstructive condition of covetousness, the practitioner cultivates four types of *dāna* pāramitā:

(1) The Wealth-Relinquishing Perfection of Giving

In the case of the first, one realizes that the breath is empty, that it is non-self, and that apart from the breath, there is no self, either. Having failed to discover any self at all, [one contemplates], "Just what is it then which is supplied and provided for by all of this stored-up material wealth?" At this time, the covetous mind (the mind inclined towards convenience)[5] immediately and naturally ceases. One then relinquishes even precious treasures just as if one were ridding oneself of snot or spittle.

One should realize that achieving an utterly penetrative understanding of the nature of the breath is the very basis of the wealth-giving form of *dāna* pāramitā.

(2) The Body-Relinquishing Perfection of Giving

Additionally, the bodhisattva realizes that there is no [inherently-existent] nature in the body, that the breath and all of the other related dharmas do not constitute a body, and that apart from the

简体字	正體字
息等法。亦无别身。尔时知身非身。即破悭身之执。既不悭于身。即能以身为奴仆给使。如法施与前人。当知了知息非息。即能具足成就舍身檀波罗蜜。复次行者。若能了息性空。不见即息是命离息有命。既不得命。破性命心。尔时即能舍命。给施众生。心无惊畏。当知了达息空。即能具足舍命檀波罗蜜。复次行者。若达息空。即不见阴入界等诸法。亦不见世间出世间种种法相。为破众生种种横计。迷执诸法轮迴六趣。故有所说。而实无说无示。以听者无闻无得故。是	息等法。亦無別身。爾時知身非身。即破慳身之執。既不慳於身。即能以身為奴僕給使。如法施與前人。當知了知息非息。即能具足成就捨身檀波羅蜜。復次行者。若能了息性空。不見即息是命離息有命。既不得命。破性命心。爾時即能捨命。給施眾生。心無驚畏。當知了達息空。即能具足捨命檀波羅蜜。復次行者。若達息空。即不見陰入界等諸法。亦不見世間出世間種種法相。為破眾生種種橫計。迷執諸法輪迴六趣。故有所說。而實無說無示。以聽者無聞無得故。是

breath and other such dharmas, there is no separately existing body, either. At this time, one realizes that the body is really just a non-body.

Consequently one immediately demolishes the attachment fundamental to any covetousness with respect to the body. Since one is no longer covetous with respect to the body, one then becomes able to employ the body in the role of a slave or servant. By doing so, one accords with Dharma in the performance of giving to whomsoever one encounters.

One should realize that in completely understanding the breath as non-breath one then immediately becomes able to completely perfect the body-relinquishing form of *dāna* pāramitā.

(3) The Life-Sacrificing Perfection of Giving

Additionally, if the practitioner is able to completely understand that the nature of the breath is emptiness, he does not perceive the breath as identical with a lifespan. Nor does he perceive that there exists any lifespan apart from the breath, either. Having been unable to discover [any ultimate existence of] a lifespan, he demolishes the thought which assumes the existence of a lifespan characterized by any [inherently-existent] nature. [553c] At this time, one immediately becomes able to relinquish one's life as a gift to furnish the needs of beings and is able to do so with a mind free of fearfulness.

One should realize that, in achieving a completely penetrative understanding of the emptiness of the breath, one immediately becomes able to perfect the life-relinquishing form of *dāna* pāramitā.

(4) The Dharma-Relinquishing Perfection of Giving

Additionally, if the practitioner achieves a penetrating understanding of the emptiness of the breath, he then no longer perceives [the inherent existence of] the aggregates, the sense bases, the sense realms, or any other such dharmas, nor does he perceive [the inherent existence of] the characteristics of any of the various sorts of worldly or supramundane dharmas, either.

[The practitioner] does have that which he proclaims in order to refute the various sorts of baseless imputations clung to by beings [which lead them to] deludedly seize upon dharmas and course along in cyclic existence within the six destinies. However, in actuality, there is nothing proclaimed and nothing explained, for the hearer of it has nothing heard and nothing gained thereby. At this

时虽行法施。不执法施。无恩于彼。而利一切。譬如大地虚空日月利益世间。而无心于物不求恩报菩萨达息性空。行平等法施檀波罗蜜。利益众生。亦复如是。当知菩萨知息性空。不得悭度而能了了分别悭度。以不可得故。知息性空。具足尸罗羼提毘梨耶禅那般若波罗蜜。亦复如是。是中应一一广旋转诸波罗蜜相。为求佛道善男子善女人。开示分别。是即略说于数息门中。修旋转陀罗尼菩萨所行无碍方便。菩萨若入是门。直说数息调心。穷劫不尽。况复于随止观还净等。种种诸禅。智惠神通。四辩力无所畏。诸地行愿。	時雖行法施。不執法施。無恩於彼。而利一切。譬如大地虛空日月利益世間。而無心於物不求恩報菩薩達息性空。行平等法施檀波羅蜜。利益眾生。亦復如是。當知菩薩知息性空。不得慳度而能了了分別慳度。以不可得故。知息性空。具足尸羅羼提毘梨耶禪那般若波羅蜜。亦復如是。是中應一一廣旋轉諸波羅蜜相。為求佛道善男子善女人。開示分別。是即略說於數息門中。修旋轉陀羅尼菩薩所行無礙方便。菩薩若入是門。直說數息調心。窮劫不盡。況復於隨止觀還淨等。種種諸禪。智惠神通。四辯力無所畏。諸地行願。
简体字	正體字

time, although one practices the giving of Dharma, one does not possess any attachment to the giving of Dharma. There is no [calculated] kindness towards others and yet one nonetheless provides benefit to everyone.

This is analogous to the great earth, empty space, and the sun and moon which provide benefit to the world and yet are free of any intentional regard for creatures and which do not seek anything in return for their kindnesses. Just so is the bodhisattva who gains a penetrating understanding of the emptiness of breath and then benefits beings through *dāna* pāramitā in the form of uniformly-offered Dharma giving.

b) Summation Regarding the Perfection of Giving

One should realize that in the bodhisattva's understanding that the nature of the breath is emptiness, he does not apprehend either covetousness or the perfections and yet he is able to completely and utterly understand and make distinctions with regard to covetousness and the perfections.

2) Summation Regarding the Other Perfections

Because it cannot be apprehended at all, he realizes the nature of the breath is emptiness. Hence his perfection of the other pāramitās of *śīla, kṣānti, vīrya,* dhyāna, and prajñā is just the same [as with the perfection of giving]. [Ideally], one should engage herein in an expansive demonstration of the implications of the "reversed" orientation in relation to the characteristic features of all of the pāramitās, opening up, explaining, and making distinctions for those sons and daughters of good family who seek to course along in the path to buddhahood.

C. Summation Regarding Cultivation of the "Reversed" Orientation

This has been a summary explanation, carried out within the gateway of counting the breaths, of the bodhisattva's practice of unobstructed skillful means as he cultivates the *dhāraṇī* of the "reversed" orientation. In the case of a bodhisattva who enters this gateway, if one were merely to discuss his training of the mind as he counts the breaths, even using up an entire kalpa, one would still not come to the end of [such a discussion]. How much the less would one be able to come to the end of the implications of the reversed orientation in making distinctions with regard to all of the different types of dhyāna, wisdom, spiritual superknowledges, the four types of eloquence, the powers, the fearlessnesses, the practices and vows

一切种智。无尽一切功德。旋转分别而可尽乎	一切種智。無盡一切功德。旋轉分別而可盡乎
简体字	正體字

on all of the grounds, the knowledge of all modes, and all of the meritorious qualities as they relate to following, stabilization, contemplation, turning, and purification.

简体字	正體字
[0553c20] 次释第八观心六妙门。观心六妙门者。此为大根性行人善识法恶。不由次第悬照诸法之源。何等为诸法之源。所谓众生心也。一切万法由心而起。若能反观心性不可得心源。即知万法皆无根本。约此观心说六妙门。非如前也。所以者何。如行者初学观心时。知一切世间出世间诸数量法。皆悉从心出。离心之外更无一法。是则数一切法。皆悉约心故数。当知心者。即是数门。复次行者。当观心时。知一切数量之法。悉随心王。若无心王。即无心数。心王动故。心数亦动。	**[0553c20]** 次釋第八觀心六妙門。觀心六妙門者。此為大根性行人善識法惡。不由次第懸照諸法之源。何等為諸法之源。所謂眾生心也。一切萬法由心而起。若能反觀心性不可得心源。即知萬法皆無根本。約此觀心說六妙門。非如前也。所以者何。如行者初學觀心時。知一切世間出世間諸數量法。皆悉從心出。離心之外更無一法。是則數一切法。皆悉約心故數。當知心者。即是數門。復次行者。當觀心時。知一切數量之法。悉隨心王。若無心王。即無心數。心王動故。心數亦動。

Chapter Eight

The Six Gates According to Contemplation of Mind

VIII. Six Gates Cultivation According to Contemplation of Mind

A. Clarification of "Contemplation of Mind's" Meaning

As for the six gates to the sublime according to "contemplation of mind," this refers to the skillful recognition of unwholesome aspects of dharmas as carried out by the practitioner whose very nature is informed by possession of great root faculties.[1] Without depending on any particular sequence, he is able to illuminate from an elevated perspective the very source of all dharmas. What is it that constitutes "the very source of all dharmas"? It is the so-called "mind of beings." All of the myriad dharmas arise from the mind. If one is able to turn back and contemplate the nature of the mind itself, then one is unable to apprehend [any inherently existent] source of the mind. One then realizes that the myriad dharmas are all entirely devoid of any fundamental foundation.

When according with this "contemplation of the mind" in explaining the six gates to the sublime, it is not the case that [this practice] is similar to what we have treated earlier. How is this so?

1. Contemplation of Mind and the Gateway of "Counting"

Take for example when one first begins to study contemplation of the mind. One realizes that all of the worldly and supramundane methods for "enumeration" all come forth entirely from the mind and that, apart from the mind, there does not exist even one single additional dharma. This being the case, then, in enumerating all dharmas, in every case it is an instance of enumeration done in concert with the mind. One should realize that it is the mind itself which constitutes the gateway of "counting."

2. Contemplation of Mind and the Gateway of "Following"

Additionally, at that very time when the practitioner contemplates the mind, he realizes that all dharmas associated with counting follow along with the "mind king."[2] If there were no mind king, then there would be no mental-factor (*caitasika*) dharmas. **[554a]** It is because there is movement in the domain of the mind king that mental-factor dharmas also move.

简体字	正體字
譬如百官臣民悉皆随顺大	譬如百官臣民悉皆隨順大
王。一切诸数量法依随心	王。一切諸數量法依隨心
王。亦复如是。如是观	王。亦復如是。如是觀
时。即知心是随门。复次	時。即知心是隨門。復次
行者。当观心时。知心性	行者。當觀心時。知心性
常寂即诸法亦寂寂故不	常寂即諸法亦寂寂故不
念。不念故即不动。不动	念。不念故即不動。不動
故名止也。当知心者即是	故名止也。當知心者即是
止门。复次行者。当观心	止門。復次行者。當觀心
时。觉了心性犹如虚空。	時。覺了心性猶如虛空。
无名无相一切语言道断。	無名無相一切語言道斷。
开无明藏。见真实性。于	開無明藏。見真實性。於
一切诸法得无着惠。当知	一切諸法得無著惠。當知
心者即是观门。复次行	心者即是觀門。復次行
者。当观心时。既不得所	者。當觀心時。既不得所
观之心。亦不得能观之	觀之心。亦不得能觀之
智。尔时心如虚空无所依	智。爾時心如虛空無所依
倚。以无着妙惠。虽不见	倚。以無著妙惠。雖不見
诸法。而还通达一切诸	諸法。而還通達一切諸
法。分别显示。入诸法界	法。分別顯示。入諸法界
无所缺减普现色身。垂形	無所缺減普現色身。垂形
九	九

This is analogous to the hundred ministers and subjects who all follow along and accord with a great king. The reliance upon and according with the mind king which takes place on the part of all of the mental-factor dharmas is just the same in this respect. At that very time when one contemplates in this way, one realizes that it is the mind itself which constitutes the gateway of "following."

3. Contemplation of Mind and the Gateway of "Stabilization"

Additionally, at the very moment when the practitioner contemplates the mind, he realizes that the nature of the mind is in a state of eternal quiescence and that this is just a case of all dharmas abiding in quiescence as well. Because they abide in a state of quiescence, he does not bear them in mind. Because he does not bear them in mind, then he does not move. Because he does not move, this constitutes "stabilization." One should realize that it is the mind itself which constitutes the gateway of "stabilization."

4. Contemplation of Mind and the Gateway of "Contemplation"

Additionally, at that very time when the practitioner contemplates the mind, he becomes completely aware that the nature of the mind is like empty space, is devoid of name, is devoid of any [inherently-existent] characteristic features, and is such that it cuts off the path of all discourse [attempting to describe it]. He opens up "the repository of ignorance" and perceives its genuine nature. He gains unattached wisdom with respect to all dharmas. One should realize that it is the mind itself which constitutes the gateway of "contemplation."

5. Contemplation of Mind and the Gateway of "Turning"

Additionally, at that very time when the practitioner contemplates the mind, since he does not apprehend [any inherent existence of] that mind which is the object of contemplation, he does not apprehend that wisdom which is able to engage in contemplation, either. At that very time, the mind is like empty space and has nothing upon which it depends.

Although he does not perceive [the inherent existence] of any dharma, employing the sublime wisdom of non-attachment, he nonetheless "turns back" and, with a penetrating understanding of all dharmas, makes distinctions about them, reveals them, and explains them. He enters the entire Dharma realm with no place being left out or only meagerly attended to. He manifests form bodies everywhere, taking on forms below in the [other] nine karmic

道。入变通藏。集诸善根。迴向菩提。庄严佛道。当知心者即是还门。复次行者。当观心时。虽不得心及诸法。而能了了分别一切诸法。虽分别一切法。不着一切法。成就一切法。不染一切法以自性清净。从本以来。不为无明惑倒之所染故。故经云。心不染烦恼。烦恼不染心。行者通达自性清净心故。入于垢法。不为垢法所染。故名为净。当知心者即是净门。如是六门。不由次第。直观心性即便具足也	道。入變通藏。集諸善根。迴向菩提。莊嚴佛道。當知心者即是還門。復次行者。當觀心時。雖不得心及諸法。而能了了分別一切諸法。雖分別一切法。不著一切法。成就一切法。不染一切法以自性清淨。從本以來。不為無明惑倒之所染故。故經云。心不染煩惱。煩惱不染心。行者通達自性清淨心故。入於垢法。不為垢法所染。故名為淨。當知心者即是淨門。如是六門。不由次第。直觀心性即便具足也
简体字	正體字

destinies.[3] He enters into the treasury of supernatural transformations and superknowledges, accumulates all manner of roots of goodness, dedicates them to bodhi through transference [of merit], and carries on with the adornment of the buddhalands. One should realize that it is the mind itself which constitutes the gateway of "turning."[4]

6. Contemplation of Mind and the Gateway of "Purification"

Additionally, at that very time when the practitioner contemplates the mind, although he is unable to apprehend [any inherent existence in] either the mind or any other dharma, still, he is able, utterly and completely, to make distinctions with regard to all dharmas. Although he makes distinctions with regard to all dharmas, he is not attached to any dharma, and thus he perfects all dharmas.

He does not become "stained" by any dharma because his very nature is pure. This is because, from the very beginning on through to the present, he has remained unstained by ignorance, delusion, or inverted views. Thus it is that a sutra says, "The mind does not become stained even in the midst of the afflictions. The afflictions do not stain the mind."[5]

Because the practitioner possesses a penetrating understanding of the purity of his own nature, even when entering into defiled dharmas, he remains unstained by defiled dharmas. Thus it is that this qualifies as "purification." One should realize that it is the mind itself which constitutes the gateway of "purification."

B. Summation of the Six Gates and Contemplation of Mind

The six gates taken up in this manner do not rely upon any sequence. One directly contemplates the nature of mind and then straightaway achieves perfection.

[0554a23] 次释第九圆观六妙门。夫圆观者。岂得如上所说。但观心源。具足六妙门。观馀诸法不得尔乎。今行者观一心。见一切心及一切法。观一法见一切法及一切心。观菩提。见一切烦恼生死。观烦恼生死。见一切菩提涅盘。观一佛见一切众生及诸佛。观一众生。见一切佛及一切众生。一切皆如影现。非内非外。不一不异。十方不可思议。本性自尔无能作者。非但于一心中。分别一切十方法界凡圣色心诸法数量。亦能于一微尘中。通达一切十方世界诸佛凡圣色心数量法门。是即略说圆观数门。	[0554a23] 次釋第九圓觀六妙門。夫圓觀者。豈得如上所說。但觀心源。具足六妙門。觀餘諸法不得爾乎。今行者觀一心。見一切心及一切法。觀一法見一切法及一切心。觀菩提。見一切煩惱生死。觀煩惱生死。見一切菩提涅槃。觀一佛見一切眾生及諸佛。觀一眾生。見一切佛及一切眾生。一切皆如影現。非內非外。不一不異。十方不可思議。本性自爾無能作者。非但於一心中。分別一切十方法界凡聖色心諸法數量。亦能於一微塵中。通達一切十方世界諸佛凡聖色心數量法門。是即略說圓觀數門。
简体字	正體字

Chapter Nine

The Six Gates According to the Perfect Contemplation

IX. Six Gates Cultivation According to the Perfect Contemplation

Now, as for the "perfect contemplation," how could it be similar to that which has been explained above wherein one only contemplated the mind's source and so perfected the six gates to the sublime and yet, in contemplating other dharmas, failed to be able to have it be so?

A. "Counting" in Accordance with the Perfect Contemplation

Now, the practitioner contemplates any single manifestation of mind and yet perceives all manifestations of mind as well as all dharmas. He contemplates but a single dharma and yet perceives all dharmas as well as all manifestations of mind. He contemplates bodhi and yet perceives all instances of affliction and birth-and-death. He contemplates affliction and birth-and-death and yet perceives all instances of bodhi and nirvāṇa. He contemplates but a single buddha and yet perceives all beings as well as all buddhas. He contemplates but a single being and yet perceives all buddhas as well as all beings.

In every case, everything manifests like reflections which do not abide either inwardly or outwardly and which are neither singular nor differentiated. [554b] Throughout the ten directions, everything is [recognized as] inconceivable and ineffable. The original nature is naturally so. There is no one who could create such circumstances.

It is not merely that, within a single thought, one distinguishes the number of all form and mind dharmas of all common persons and āryas throughout the Dharma realm's ten directions. Rather, one is also able, even within a single dust mote, to command a penetrating comprehension of all dharmic methods of enumeration belonging to all buddhas throughout the worlds of the ten directions as they pertain to the forms and minds of all common persons and āryas.

B. The Similar character of the Other Five Gates

This then is a summary description of the gateway of counting as it occurs within the perfect contemplation. The [gateways] of

随止观还净等。一一皆亦如是。是数微妙不可思议非口所宣。非心所测。尚非诸小菩萨及一乘境界。况诸凡夫。若有利根大士闻如是无法。能信解受持。正念思惟。专精修习。当知。是人行佛行处。住佛住处。入如来室。着如来衣。坐如来座。即于此身。必定当得六根清净。开佛知见。普现色身。成等正觉。故华严经云。初发心时便成正觉。了达诸法真实之性。所有惠身不由他悟	隨止觀還淨等。一一皆亦如是。是數微妙不可思議非口所宣。非心所測。尚非諸小菩薩及一乘境界。況諸凡夫。若有利根大士聞如是無法。能信解受持。正念思惟。專精修習。當知。是人行佛行處。住佛住處。入如來室。著如來衣。坐如來座。即於此身。必定當得六根清淨。開佛知見。普現色身。成等正覺。故華嚴經云。初發心時便成正覺。了達諸法真實之性。所有惠身不由他悟
简体字	正體字

following, stabilization, contemplation, turning, and purification, are in each and every case similar to this. This [level of engaging the practice of] counting is itself so subtle, sublime, inconceivable, and ineffable that it cannot be proclaimed in words or fathomed by the mind. Not even the lesser bodhisattvas would be able to reach to this One-Vehicle realm of perception, how much the less would this be possible for any common person.

C. The Relationship of Such Practitioners to the Tathāgata

If it were to happen that there was some great eminence with sharp faculties who, when he heard such a sublime[1] dharma as this, was then able to believe in, understand, and uphold it, deliberating upon it with right mindfulness, and cultivating it with deeply-committed diligence—one should know that this person is one who carries on his practice in the Buddha's place of practice and dwells in the Buddha's dwelling place. He "enters the room of the Tathāgata, dons the robe of the Tathāgata, and sits upon the throne of the Tathāgata."[2]

D. The Impending Realizations of Such Practitioners

He will definitely, in this very body, succeed in gaining the purification of the six sense faculties and in opening forth the knowledge and vision of the Buddha. He will be able to universally manifest form bodies and achieve the equal and right enlightenment. Thus it is that the *Floral Adornment Sutra* states, "At the very time of generating the aspiration, one then succeeds in achieving the right enlightenment. He gains a penetrating comprehension of the genuine nature of all dharmas and completely [perfects] the wisdom body, achieving this awakening with no reliance on others."[3]

[0554b14] 次释第十证相六妙门。前九种六妙门。皆修因之相。义兼证果。说不具足。今当更分别六妙门证相。六门有四种一者次第证。二者互证。三者旋转证。四者圆顿证。云何次第证。如上第一历别对诸禅门。及次第相生六妙门中已略说。次第证相细寻自知。今不别说第二互证。此约第三随便宜。第四对治。第五相摄。第六通观。四种妙门中论证相。所以者何。此四种妙门修行方便。无定次第。故证亦复迴互不定。	[0554b14] 次釋第十證相六妙門。前九種六妙門。皆修因之相。義兼證果。說不具足。今當更分別六妙門證相。六門有四種一者次第證。二者互證。三者旋轉證。四者圓頓證。云何次第證。如上第一歷別對諸禪門。及次第相生六妙門中已略說。次第證相細尋自知。今不別說第二互證。此約第三隨便宜。第四對治。第五相攝。第六通觀。四種妙門中論證相。所以者何。此四種妙門修行方便。無定次第。故證亦復迴互不定。
简体字	正體字

Chapter Ten

The Six Gates According to the Signs of Realization

X. Six Gates Cultivation According to the Signs of Realization

The previous nine categories of the six gates to the sublime have all been concerned with the characteristic features of cultivating the causes. Their meanings have implications with regard to the realization of the fruits. This has not yet been completely explained. Now, however, we shall proceed with making distinctions regarding the characteristic features of realization associated with the six gates to the sublime.

When taking up this topic as it relates to the six gates, there are four categories involved. The first is sequential realization. The second is interrelated realization. The third is reverse-oriented realization. The fourth is perfect-and-sudden realization.

A. First, Sequential Realization

What is meant by "sequential" realization? This is as already briefly discussed in the [first] chapter, "The Six Gates in Correlation with the Dhyānas" and also in the next chapter, "The Six Gates to the Sublime in Accordance with Sequential Development." If one deliberates with attention to the subtle details, one will realize for himself what is involved in the characteristic features of sequential realization. Hence we will not now take up a separate discussion of the matter.

B. Second, Interrelated Realization

1. Relevant Concepts

As for the second, "interrelated realization," this refers to the characteristic features of [cultivation and] realization discussed in four of the previous chapters on the gates to the sublime, in particular the third which is devoted to suitability and appropriateness, the fourth which is devoted to counteraction, the fifth which is devoted to mutual inclusiveness, and the sixth, [in its subsection] devoted to contemplations in the sphere of "identities."

How is this [concept applicable here]? The skillful means taken up in the cultivation of these four categories within the gates to the sublime involve no fixed sequence, hence the realizations are also not fixed in their respective relationships with each other.

如行者当数息时。发十六触等诸暗证隐没无记有垢等法。此禅即是数息证相之体。而今不定。或有行者。于数息中。见身毛孔虚疎。彻见三十六物。当知于数息中。证于随门。复有行者。于数息中。证空静定。以觉身心。寂然无所缘念。入此定时。虽复浅深有殊而皆是空寂之相。当知于数息中证止门禅定也。复次行者。当数息时。内外死尸。不净膖胀烂坏。及白骨光明等。定心安隐。当知于数息中。证观门禅也。	如行者當數息時。發十六觸等諸闇證隱沒無記有垢等法。此禪即是數息證相之體。而今不定。或有行者。於數息中。見身毛孔虛疎。徹見三十六物。當知於數息中。證於隨門。復有行者。於數息中。證空靜定。以覺身心。寂然無所緣念。入此定時。雖復淺深有殊而皆是空寂之相。當知於數息中證止門禪定也。復次行者。當數息時。內外死屍。不淨膖脹爛壞。及白骨光明等。定心安隱。當知於數息中。證觀門禪也。
简体字	正體字

2. Inter-related Realizations Linked to "Counting"

a. Realizations within the Sphere of "Counting"

Take for example those times when the practitioner is engaged in counting the breaths and then, as he generates the sixteen kinds of sensations and such,[1] there then manifest the various dharmas associated with the obscure realizations, submergence, non-recollection, and defilement.[2] These sorts of dhyāna meditation states are signs substantially linked to the process of bringing the counting of the breaths to realization. However, it is not a fixed matter [precisely what will manifest] just now [as one cultivates the counting of the breaths].

b. Realization of "Following" While "Counting"

[For example], there are some practitioners who, even while counting the breaths, observe it emptily moving through the pores of the body or who, with penetrating vision, directly view the thirty-six parts of their body. One should realize that this is a case of achieving realization of the gateway of "following" even while engaged in counting the breaths.

c. Realization of "Stabilization" While "Counting"

Additionally, there are also those practitioners who, even while counting the breaths, gain realization of an empty and still absorption through which they become aware of the body and mind as quiescent and in which nothing whatsoever is taken as an objective condition or borne in mind. When one enters this absorption, although there are differences in the depth of it, in every case, it is characterized by emptiness and stillness. One should realize that this is a case of realizing a dhyāna absorption associated with the gateway of "stabilization" even while engaged in counting the breaths. **[554c]**

d. Realization of "Contemplation" While "Counting"

Then again, there are also those practitioners who, even while counting the breaths, see [images of] their own and others' corpses, the signs of impurity, the swollen and distended corpse, the rotting and deteriorating corpse, and the others on through to the white skeleton which radiates light,[3] and so forth, with the mind of absorption remaining peaceful and stable. One should know that this is an instance of realizing dhyāna associated with the gateway of "contemplation" even while engaged in counting the breaths.

简体字	正體字
复次行者。当数息时。发空无相智慧三十七品四谛十二因缘等巧惠方便。思觉心起。破折诸法。反本还源。当知于数息中。证还门禅也。复次行者。或于数息之时。身心寂然。不得诸法。妄垢不生。分别不起。心想寂然。明识法相。无所依倚当知于数息中证净门禅也。此则略说于数息中。互发六门禅相。前后不定。未必悉如今说。馀随止观还净。一一互证诸禅相亦如是。所以有此互证诸禅者。意有二种一者修诸禅时互修故。发亦随互。意如	復次行者。當數息時。發空無相智慧三十七品四諦十二因緣等巧惠方便。思覺心起。破折諸法。反本還源。當知於數息中。證還門禪也。復次行者。或於數息之時。身心寂然。不得諸法。妄垢不生。分別不起。心想寂然。明識法相。無所依倚當知於數息中證淨門禪也。此則略說於數息中。互發六門禪相。前後不定。未必悉如今說。餘隨止觀還淨。一一互證諸禪相亦如是。所以有此互證諸禪者。意有二種一者修諸禪時互修故。發亦隨互。意如

e. Realization of "Turning" While "Counting"

Then again, there are also those practitioners who, even while engaged in counting the breaths, generate the wisdom associated with emptiness and signlessness, with the thirty-seven wings of enlightenment, with the four truths, with the twelve causes and conditions, and other such clever and wise skillful means. The mind of deliberation and awareness arises and engages in the deconstructing analysis of dharmas. In doing so, one turns back towards the origin and returns to the source. One should realize that this is an instance of realizing dhyāna associated with the gateway of "turning," even while engaged in counting the breaths.

f. Realization of "Purification" While "Counting"

Then again, there may be some instances where a practitioner, even while engaged in counting the breaths, experiences the body and mind abiding in a state of stillness. He does not apprehend any dharma, falseness and defilement do not arise, and discriminations do not occur. Even though the mind remains in a state of stillness, he possesses clear awareness of the characteristics of dharmas and has nothing upon which he relies. One should realize that this is an instance of realizing dhyāna associated with the gateway of "purification" even while engaged in counting the breaths.

3. Summation on Inter-related Realization Specific to the Six Gates

This then has been a summary discussion of interrelated generation of the signs of dhyāna associated with the six gates even while engaged in counting the breaths. The actual sequence of what comes before and what comes later is unfixed. It is not necessarily the case that all instances will accord with this present description.

In the case of the other [five gates] of following, stabilization, contemplation, turning, and purification, in each and every case the signs of interrelated realization of dhyāna accord with this [example case above].

4. The Two Bases Underlying Interrelated Realization

The bases for these instances of interrelated realizations of dhyāna are two-fold, as follows:

a. First, Conjoint Cultivation of Different Practices

In the case of the first, it may be that, because one is engaged in inter-related cultivation of particular sorts of dhyāna meditations, the generation [of realizations] occurs then in a correspondingly interrelated manner as well. The relevant concepts accord with the

前四种修六妙门相。二者宿世业缘善根发。是故互发不定。义如坐禅内方便验善恶根性中广说。第三云何名证旋转六妙门相。此的依第七旋转修故发。所谓证相者。即有二种。一者证旋转解。二者证旋转行。云何名为证旋转解发相。行者于数息中。巧惠旋转修习故。尔时或证深禅定。或说浅定。于此等定中。豁然心惠开发。旋转觉识。解真无碍。不由心念。任运旋转。觉识法门。	前四種修六妙門相。二者宿世業緣善根發。是故互發不定。義如坐禪內方便驗善惡根性中廣說。第三云何名證旋轉六妙門相。此的依第七旋轉修故發。所謂證相者。即有二種。一者證旋轉解。二者證旋轉行。云何名為證旋轉解發相。行者於數息中。巧惠旋轉修習故。爾時或證深禪定。或說淺定。於此等定中。豁然心惠開發。旋轉覺識。解真無礙。不由心念。任運旋轉。覺識法門。
简体字	正體字

characteristic features of Six-Gates practice treated in the four previously-mentioned [Chapters Three through Six which discussed suitability, counteraction, mutual-inclusion, and "identities"].[4]

b. Second, Previous-Life Causal Factors

Second, it may be on account of the development of roots of goodness associated with past life karmic conditions that there occur interrelated manifestations arising in an unfixed manner. The meaning of this corresponds to the extensive discussion in the [*Essentials for Practicing Calming-and-Insight and*] *Dhyāna Meditation,* in the section devoted to distinguishing manifestations of roots of goodness from manifestations of roots of unwholesome karma as one utilizes inwardly-focused skillful means.[5]

C. Third, Reverse-Oriented Realization

As for the third category, what are the signs of realization in reverse-oriented cultivation of the six gates to the sublime? These depend for their generation directly on pursuit of the [reverse-oriented] cultivation discussed in the seventh chapter.

1. The Two Categories of Reverse-Oriented Realization Signs

As for the so-called "signs of realization," they are of two types:

First, those occurring upon realization of the comprehension associated with reverse-oriented cultivation.

Second, those occurring upon realization of the practices associated with reverse-oriented cultivation.

a. Signs of Realization in Reverse-Oriented Comprehension

What are the signs generated upon realizing the comprehension associated with reverse-oriented cultivation? Even while engaged in the counting of the breaths, on account of clever and wise cultivation of reverse-oriented practice, at that very time, the practitioner may achieve realization of deep levels of dhyāna absorption or, alternately, may achieve realization[6] of shallow levels of dhyāna absorption.

While in the midst of these absorptions, as if achieving a sudden breaking through, there occurs the opening up and generation of that awakened consciousness associated with reverse-oriented practice wherein one's comprehension of the truth becomes unobstructed. With no reliance upon thoughts in the mind, one carries forward with reverse-oriented practice while abiding in a state of awakened comprehension of the gateways to Dharma.

旋转有二种。一者总相旋转解。二者别相。总相复有二种。一者解真总相。二者解俗总相。别相复有二种。一者解真别相。二者解俗别相。于一总相法中。旋转解一切法。别相亦尔。云何名为证旋转行相。行者如所解。心不违言。心口相应。法门现前。心行坚固。任运增长。不由念力。诸善功德自生。诸恶自息。总相别相皆如上说。但有相应之异。入诸法门境界显现之殊故。今则略出证旋转行。如一数门。具二种证旋转故馀随止观还净亦如是。	旋轉有二種。一者總相旋轉解。二者別相。總相復有二種。一者解真總相。二者解俗總相。別相復有二種。一者解真別相。二者解俗別相。於一總相法中。旋轉解一切法。別相亦爾。云何名為證旋轉行相。行者如所解。心不違言。心口相應。法門現前。心行堅固。任運增長。不由念力。諸善功德自生。諸惡自息。總相別相皆如上說。但有相應之異。入諸法門境界顯現之殊故。今則略出證旋轉行。如一數門。具二種證旋轉故餘隨止觀還淨亦如是。
简体字	正體字

Comprehension associated with reverse-oriented practice is of two types:

First, the reverse-oriented practice comprehension which understands general characteristics.

Second, [the reverse-oriented practice comprehension which understands] specific characteristics.

Comprehension of general characteristics is, in turn, also of two types: First, comprehension of the general characteristics of that which is true. Second, comprehension of the general characteristics of that which is mundane.

Comprehension of specific characteristics is, in turn, also of two types: First, comprehension of the specific characteristics of that which is true. Second, comprehension of the specific characteristics of that which is mundane.

Even when relating only to the dharma of a single general characteristic, one's reverse-oriented practice comprehension is able to extend to all dharmas. The circumstance is the same with regard to specific characteristics.

b. Signs Generated on Realization of Reverse-Oriented Practices

What are the signs of realizing the practices associated with reverse-oriented cultivation? The practitioner's actions accord with his comprehension. His mind does not contradict what he says. His mind and his mouth are in mutual accord. The gateways to Dharma manifest right before him. His mind and actions are solid and resolute, spontaneously progressing in a manner which brings increasing development. He does not [have any need to] resort to the power of thought. Every form of meritorious quality naturally arises in him. Every form of unwholesomeness naturally ceases in him.

The situation in regard to both general characteristics and specific characteristics is as described above. Differences exist only as adaptations corresponding [to particular circumstances]. [555a] These occur on account of specific differences in the way objective circumstances manifest when entering the various Dharma gateways.

Now we shall set forth herein only a summary description of [the signs of realization] linked to reverse-oriented practice. Just as the one gateway of counting may completely embody two categories of reverse-oriented realization, so too may this occur in relation to the other gateways of following, stabilization, contemplation, turning, and purification.

略说不具足者。自善思惟。取意广对诸法门也。证旋转六妙门者。即是得旋陀罗尼门也。是名无碍辩才巧惠方便遮诸恶令不得起。持诸功德令不漏失。任是法门。必定不久入菩萨位。成就阿耨多罗三藐三菩提也。第四云何名为圆证六妙门。行者因第八观心。第九圆观。二种六妙门为方便。是观成时。即便发圆证也。证有二种。一者解证无碍巧惠不由心念。自然圆证识法界故名解证。二者会证妙惠朗然开发。明照法界通达无碍也。证相有二种。一者相似证相。如法华经中明六根清净相。	略說不具足者。自善思惟。取意廣對諸法門也。證旋轉六妙門者。即是得旋陀羅尼門也。是名無礙辯才巧惠方便遮諸惡令不得起。持諸功德令不漏失。任是法門。必定不久入菩薩位。成就阿耨多羅三藐三菩提也。第四云何名為圓證六妙門。行者因第八觀心。第九圓觀。二種六妙門為方便。是觀成時。即便發圓證也。證有二種。一者解證無礙巧惠不由心念。自然圓證識法界故名解證。二者會證妙惠朗然開發。明照法界通達無礙也。證相有二種。一者相似證相。如法華經中明六根清淨相。
简体字	正體字

As for whatever is incompletely described in this brief explanation, one may skillfully deliberate upon it for himself, taking up the ideas and engaging in an extensive matching to all of the entryways into the Dharma.

The realization of reverse-oriented practice of the six gates to the sublime is essentially identical to realizing entry into the "turning-around" *dhāraṇī* gateway. This brings with it unobstructed eloquence in speech, the clever and wise implementation of skillful means, the blocking off of evil actions and prevention of their arising, and the upholding of all meritorious qualities so that they are prevented from slipping away. Whensoever one gains command of this gateway to Dharma, he will before long definitely enter into "the station of [irreversible] bodhisattvahood" and will succeed in perfecting *anuttarasamyaksaṃbodhi.*

D. Fourth, Perfect Realization

As for the fourth, what is meant by "perfect realization" of the six gates to the sublime? The cause for it lies in the practitioner's taking as skillful means two of the [ten approaches to cultivating] the six gates to the sublime: number eight, "contemplation of the mind," and number nine, the "perfect contemplation." When these contemplations are perfected, one then generates perfect realization.

1. Realization Related to Comprehension

This realization is of two types: The first is "realization related to comprehension." This is characterized by unobstructed skillfulness in the implementation of wisdom, the arising of which does not depend on thought processes in the mind. It is because one naturally and perfectly realizes knowing awareness of the Dharma realm that it is referred to as "realization related to comprehension."

2. All-Encompassing Realization

The second type is "all-encompassing realization." Sublime wisdom opens forth and manifests with brightly-shining clarity, clearly illuminating the Dharma realm, manifesting unobstructedly penetrative understanding.

The characteristics of this [second type of] realization are of two kinds: The first kind involves those signs which by their very nature are a semblance of realization. These are of the sort contained in the *Lotus Sutra* where it explains the signs of purification of the six sense faculties.

简体字	正體字
二者真实证相。如华严经中明初发心圆满功德智慧相也。云何名相似圆证。为六妙门。如法华经说眼根清净中。能一时数十方凡圣色心等法数量。故名数门。一切色法。随顺于眼根。眼不违色法。共相随顺。故名随门。如是见时。眼根识寂然不动。故名止门。不以二相见诸佛国。通达无碍。善巧分别。照了法性故名观门。还于眼根境界中。通达耳鼻舌身意等诸根境界。悉明了无碍。不	二者真實證相。如華嚴經中明初發心圓滿功德智慧相也。云何名相似圓證。為六妙門。如法華經說眼根清淨中。能一時數十方凡聖色心等法數量。故名數門。一切色法。隨順於眼根。眼不違色法。共相隨順。故名隨門。如是見時。眼根識寂然不動。故名止門。不以二相見諸佛國。通達無礙。善巧分別。照了法性故名觀門。還於眼根境界中。通達耳鼻舌身意等諸根境界。悉明了無礙。不

The second kind consists of those which by their nature are signs of genuine realization. These are of the sort contained in the *Floral Adornment Sutra* where it explains the signs of perfectly complete merit and wisdom when first generating the [bodhi] mind.

a. Semblances of Perfect Realization Associated with the Six Gates

What is meant by a semblance of perfect realization as it applies to the six gates to the sublime?

1) Semblances Associated with "Counting"

This is as exemplified by the *Lotus Sutra's* description with respect to purification of the eye faculty of the ability to count in a single moment the sum of all such dharmas as the physical forms and minds of all common persons and āryas throughout the ten directions. Thus it is that we may speak of [a semblance of perfect realization within] the gateway of counting.

2) Semblances Associated with "Following"

All form dharmas accord with the eye faculty. The eye does not react against any form dharma. There is mutual accord and harmony between them. It is on account of this that we may speak of [a semblance of perfect realization within] the gateway of following.

3) Semblances Associated with "Stabilization"

It is on account of the eye faculty and its corresponding consciousness remaining still and unmoving even when engaged in seeing that we may speak of [a semblance of perfect realization within] the gateway of stabilization.

4) Semblances Associated with "Contemplation"

One views all buddhalands in a manner not reliant on dual characteristics, doing so in a way which involves unobstructedly penetrating comprehension. One skillfully and cleverly makes distinctions while utterly illuminating the very nature of dharmas. Thus it is that we may speak of [a semblance of perfect realization within] the gateway of contemplation.

5) Semblances Associated with "Turning"

One turns back [the focus of one's meditation] and, while still attending to the objective realms of the eye faculty, one is also able to penetratingly perceive the objective realms of the ear, nose, tongue, body, and mind, perceiving them all with utter and unobstructed clarity. [These six objective realms] are not perceived as

简体字	正體字
一不异相故。故名还门。复次见己眼根境界。还于十方凡圣眼界中现故。亦名为还门虽了了通达见如是事。而不起妄想分利。知本性常净无可染法。不住不着。不起法爱。故名净门。此则略说于眼根清净中。证相似六妙门相。馀五根亦如是。广说如法华经明也。云何名真实圆证六妙门。有二种。一者别对。二通对。别对者。十住为数门。十行为随门。十迴向为止门。十地所观门。等觉为还门。妙觉为净门。	一不異相故。故名還門。復次見己眼根境界。還於十方凡聖眼界中現故。亦名為還門雖了了通達見如是事。而不起妄想分利。知本性常淨無可染法。不住不著。不起法愛。故名淨門。此則略說於眼根清淨中。證相似六妙門相。餘五根亦如是。廣說如法華經明也。云何名真實圓證六妙門。有二種。一者別對。二通對。別對者。十住為數門。十行為隨門。十迴向為止門。十地所觀門。等覺為還門。妙覺為淨門。

characterized by either singularity or difference. Thus it is that we may speak of [a semblance of perfect realization within] the gateway of "turning."

Additionally, even while perceiving the objective realm of one's own eye faculty, one turns back one's contemplation so that it extends to [also include] appearances arising in the objective visual realms of the common persons and āryas throughout the ten directions. It is based on this [phenomenon] that this also qualifies as [a semblance of perfect realization within] the gateway of turning.

6) Semblances Associated with "Purification"

Although one possesses a complete and utterly penetrating perception of such phenomena, still, one does not generate erroneous thoughts or engage in making discriminations.[7] One realizes that the fundamental nature is an eternally pure dharma invulnerable to any sort of defilement. One refrains from abiding in dependence on it or becoming attached to it. One refrains from generating affection for dharmas. Thus it is that we may speak of [a semblance of perfect realization within] the gateway of purification.

This then has been a brief description of the achievement of semblances of perfect realization of the six gates to the sublime as they may occur within the realm of the purified eye faculty. The situation is very much the same in respect to the other five sense faculties. An extensive discussion would accord with the *Lotus Sutra*'s explanation of the topic.

b. Genuinely Perfect Realization

What then is meant by genuinely perfect realization of the six gates to the sublime? It is of two types. The first consists of specific correspondences. [555b] The second consists of general correspondences.

1) Specific Correspondences

As for [the first], the specific correspondences, they are as follows: The ten dwellings constitute [genuinely perfect realization of] the gateway of counting. The ten conducts constitute [genuinely perfect realization of] the gateway of following. The ten transferences constitute [genuinely perfect realization of] the gateway of stabilization. The ten grounds constitute [genuinely perfect realization of] the gateway of contemplation. Equal enlightenment constitutes [genuinely perfect realization of] the gateway of turning. Sublime enlightenment constitutes [genuinely perfect realization of] the gateway of purification.

简体字	正體字
二通对者。有三种证。一者初证二者中证。三者究竟证。初证者。有菩萨入阿字门。亦名初发心住。得真无生法忍惠。尔时能于一念心中。数不可说微尘世界诸佛菩萨声闻缘觉诸心行。及数无量法门。故名数门。能一念心中。随顺法界所有事业。故名随门。能一念心中入百千三昧及一切三昧。虚妄及习俱止息。故名为止门。能一念心中。觉了一切法相。具足种种观智惠。故名观门。能一念心中。通达诸法	二通對者。有三種證。一者初證二者中證。三者究竟證。初證者。有菩薩入阿字門。亦名初發心住。得真無生法忍惠。爾時能於一念心中。數不可說微塵世界諸佛菩薩聲聞緣覺諸心行。及數無量法門。故名數門。能一念心中。隨順法界所有事業。故名隨門。能一念心中入百千三昧及一切三昧。虛妄及習俱止息。故名為止門。能一念心中。覺了一切法相。具足種種觀智惠。故名觀門。能一念心中。通達諸法

2) General Correspondences

As for the second, the general correspondences, there are three levels of realization in this regard, as follows: First, initial-level realization. Second, intermediate-level realization. Third, ultimate-level realization.

a) Initial-Level Perfect Realization

i) Initial-Level Perfect Realization of "Counting"

As for initial-level realization, this involves a bodhisattva who enters the gateway of the "*a*" syllable, also known as "the dwelling of initial generation of [bodhi] resolve." He then realizes the wisdom linked to unproduced-dharmas patience. At that time, he is able, even in but a single thought, to enumerate all of the mental actions coursed in by all buddhas, bodhisattvas, śrāvaka disciples, and pratyekabuddhas[8] throughout world systems as numerous as an ineffable[9] number of tiny dust motes. He is also able to count the incalculable number of associated entryways to Dharma therein. It is on the basis of this that we may speak of [the initial level of genuinely perfect realization of] the gateway of counting.

ii) Initial-Level Perfect Realization of "Following"

One is able in the space of but a single thought of the mind to acquiesce in all phenomenal karma occurring throughout the Dharma realm. Thus it is that we may speak of [the initial level of genuinely perfect realization] of the gateway of following.

iii) Initial-Level Perfect Realization of "Stabilization"

One is able in the space of but a single thought of the mind to enter into a hundred thousand samādhis or even into all samādhis. One thereby halts and puts utterly to rest all falseness and residual karmic propensities. Thus it is that we may speak of [the initial level of genuinely perfect realization] of the gateway of stabilization.

iv) Initial-Level Perfect Realization of "Contemplation"

One is able in the space of but a single thought of the mind to become entirely aware of the characteristic features of all dharmas and to perfect all manner of contemplation-related forms of wisdom. Thus it is that we may speak of [the initial level of genuinely perfect realization] of the gateway of contemplation.

v) Initial-Level Perfect Realization of "Turning"

One is able in the space of but a single thought of the mind to penetratingly understand all dharmas to a degree whereby they become

了了分明。神通转变调伏	了了分明。神通轉變調伏
众生。反本还源。故名还	眾生。反本還源。故名還
门。能一念心中。成就如	門。能一念心中。成就如
上所说事。而心无染着。	上所說事。而心無染著。
不为诸法之所染污故。亦	不為諸法之所染污故。亦
能净佛国土。令众生入三	能淨佛國土。令眾生入三
乘净道。故名净门。初心	乘淨道。故名淨門。初心
菩萨入是法门。如经所	菩薩入是法門。如經所
说。亦名为佛也。已得般	說。亦名為佛也。已得般
若正惠。闻如来藏。显真	若正惠。聞如來藏。顯真
法身。具首楞严。明见佛	法身。具首楞嚴。明見佛
性。住大涅盘。入法华三	性。住大涅槃。入法華三
昧不思议一实。境界也。	昧不思議一實。境界也。
广说如华严经中所明。是	廣說如華嚴經中所明。是
为初地证不可思议真实六	為初地證不可思議真實六
妙门也。中证者。馀九	妙門也。中證者。餘九
住。十行。十迴向。十	住。十行。十迴向。十
地。等觉地。皆名中证不	地。等覺地。皆名中證不
可思议真实六妙门也。云	可思議真實六妙門也。云
何名究竟圆证六妙门。后	何名究竟圓證六妙門。後
心菩萨入荼字门。得一念	心菩薩入荼字門。得一念
相应惠。妙觉现前。	相應惠。妙覺現前。
简体字	正體字

completely and utterly distinct and clear. One is also able to employ spiritual superknowledges to turn back, employing transformations, to engage in subduing and training beings. One turns back towards the origin and returns to the source. Thus it is that we may speak of [the initial level of genuinely perfect realization] of the gateway of turning.

vi) Initial-Level Perfect Realization of "Purification"

One is able in the space of but a single thought of the mind to perfect the works as described above and yet maintain a mind free of defilement or attachment. This is because one is not defiled or sullied by any dharma. One remains able to engage in purification of the buddhalands while causing beings to enter the pure path of the Three Vehicles. Thus it is that we may speak of [the initial level of genuinely perfect realization] of the gateway of purification.

When the bodhisattva at the point of initial resolve enters this gateway to dharma, as declared in the sutras, he may also be referred to then as a buddha. He has already realized the right wisdom of prajñā. He has heard the [Dharma] treasury of the Tathāgatas. He manifests the genuine Dharma body. He perfectly embodies the foremost *śūraṅgama* [samādhi]. He clearly perceives the nature of buddhahood. He abides in the great nirvāṇa. He enters into the lotus samādhi's inconceivable and ineffable realm of realization of the singular reality.

When this is extensively explained, it is as made clear in the *Floral Adornment* (*Avataṃsaka*) *Sutra*. This is the realization of the six gates to the sublime which is inconceivable, ineffable, and genuine, precisely as it occurs at the level of the first ground (*bhūmi*).

b) Intermediate-Level Perfect Realization

As for the intermediate level of [genuine] realization, the other nine dwellings, the ten conducts, the ten transferences, the ten grounds, and the ground of equal enlightenment all qualify as subsumed within the intermediate level of that realization of the six gates to the sublime which is inconceivable, ineffable, and genuine.

c) Ultimate-Level Perfect Realization

What is it that is meant by the ultimate level of perfect realization of the six gates to the sublime? The bodhisattva at the latter stages of mind [awakening] enters into the gateway of the "*cha*" syllable and realizes the wisdom corresponding to unified mindfulness. Sublime enlightenment manifests before him. He achieves

简体字	正體字
穷照法界。于六种法门究竟通达。功用普备无所缺减。即是究竟圆满六妙门也。分别数随止观还净诸法门证相意不异前。但有圆极之殊。故璎珞经云。三贤十圣忍中行。唯佛一人能尽源。法华经言。唯佛与佛。乃能究尽诸法实相。此约修行教道。作如是说。以理而为论。法界圆通。诸佛菩萨所证法门。始终不二。故大品经言。初阿后茶其意无别。涅盘经言。发心毕竟二不别。如是二心先心难。华严经言。从初地悉具一切诸地功德。法华经言。如是本末究竟等	窮照法界。於六種法門究竟通達。功用普備無所缺減。即是究竟圓滿六妙門也。分別數隨止觀還淨諸法門證相意不異前。但有圓極之殊。故瓔珞經云。三賢十聖忍中行。唯佛一人能盡源。法華經言。唯佛與佛。乃能究盡諸法實相。此約修行教道。作如是說。以理而為論。法界圓通。諸佛菩薩所證法門。始終不二。故大品經言。初阿後茶其意無別。涅槃經言。發心畢竟二不別。如是二心先心難。華嚴經言。從初地悉具一切諸地功德。法華經言。如是本末究竟等
六妙法门一卷	六妙法門一卷

exhaustive illumination of the entire Dharma realm. He gains the most ultimate form of penetrative realization of these six sorts of Dharma gateways along with a universally replete utilization of them free of any deficiency. It is precisely this which constitutes the ultimately perfect realization of the six gates to the sublime.

The analysis of the characteristic features of realization linked to the Dharma gateways consisting in counting, following, stabilization, contemplation, turning and purification involve ideas which are not different than those described above. It is merely that there are special distinctions associated with perfect ultimacy.

i) Corroborating Scriptural Citations

Thus it is that the *Necklace Sutra* states, "As for the patience-related practices engaged in by the three levels of worthies and the ten levels of āryas—only the Buddha, that one person, is able to reach all the way to their very source."[10]

The *Lotus Sutra* says, "It is only one buddha together with another buddha who is able to exhaustively describe the true character of dharmas."[11]

This relates to the cultivation of the Path set forth by the teachings. [555c] Statements of this sort base their discourse in the noumenal reality. The perfectly penetrating understanding of the Dharma realm and the realization of Dharma gateways achieved by buddhas and bodhisattvas—from start to finish, these are not two separate matters. Thus it is that the longer-edition [*Mahā-prajñā-pāramitā*] *Sutra* states, "At the beginning, it is the *'a'* syllable. At the end it is the *'cha'* syllable. There is [ultimately] no difference as regards their meanings."[12]

The *Nirvāṇa Sutra* states, "The generation of the resolve and the ultimate [realization]—the two are not different. Of these two mind states, the former mind state is the more difficult [to develop]."[13]

The *Floral Adornment Sutra* states, "Beginning from the very first ground, there is complete embodiment of the meritorious qualities of all of the grounds."[14]

The *Lotus Sutra* states, "Thus it is that the origin and the end point are ultimately equal."[15]

The End of this Single-Fascicle Text: ***The Six Dharma Gates to the Sublime.***

Endnotes

Preface

1. This text is found in the *Taisho* canon at: T46.1917.549a2–55c7.
2. "Three Vehicles" refers to those of the Śrāvaka Disciples, the Pratyekabuddhas, and Bodhisattvas. The now-common Western lay-Buddhist ideas that they refer to Theravada, Mahāyāna, and Vajrayāna, or perhaps even less logically, to Theravada, Vajrayāna, and "Zen," are erroneous. Vehicles are defined with reference to their result: The Śrāvaka Disciples are bound for arhatship; the Pratyekabuddhas are bound for a state of solitary enlightenment resulting from observation of the twelve links of conditioned co-production; and the Bodhisattvas are destined for the utmost, right, and perfect enlightenment of a buddha (*anuttarasamyaksaṃbodhi*).
3. This refers to the Bodhi Tree at Bodhgaya in India's Bihar State.
4. *Ānāpāna* refers to the meditation technique based on mindfulness of the breath. It was recommended by the Buddha as most appropriate and effective for controlling mental discursiveness.
5. This listing of the six gates is a direct quote from a "life-of-the Buddha" scripture entitled: the *Origins Sutra on the Prince's Auspicious Response* (太子瑞應本起經 – T02.185.476c). This scripture was translated by Zhiqian between 223 and 253 CE. The parenthetically-included original Sanskrit for the six gates is per De la Valleé Poussin as supplied in his translation of *L'Abhidharmakośa de Vasubandhu*.

   This same list is discussed in the *Vibhāṣā* of Kātyāyaniputra, circa 200 BCE (T28.1546.105b29–6a01), at greater length in the *Mahā-vibhāṣā* of Vasumitra (T27.1545.134c26–35b20), and in the *Abhidharma-kośa-bhāṣyam* of Vasubandhu (Pruden, p. 922–3). Pruden references Pali scripture locations: *Dīgha*, ii.291; *Majjhima*, i.425 (p. 1049, note 89).

   Finally, Buddhaghosa's much later Pali-tradition commentary preserves the same list in a slightly altered version (*Path of Purification*, VIII: 189–225, p. 300–309).

   My point here is to demonstrate that this six-gate meditation method is *not* a later-period Mahāyāna construct, but rather a meditation cultivation formula rooted in the earliest period of Indian Buddhism. A closer examination of this formula will help us develop a much more refined view of traditional Buddhist meditation, one which goes beyond the very simplistic assumptions generally prevailing in the West which tend to look upon the tradition as consisting primarily in a very rudimentary form of *ānāpāna* (breath) meditation only later overlaid with doctrinally sophisticated calming-and-insight elaborations of the same sort as we see in this six-gate schema.

6. "Myriad practices" refers to the ten thousand subsidiary practices which, cultivated together with the six perfections for a period of three limitlessly-long eons, constitute the bodhisattva's path to buddhahood.
7. The "five-gate dhyāna" refers to absorptions based in realization of impermanence, suffering, emptiness [of inherent existence], absence of self, and quiescent extinction. In the Mahāyāna, Vimalakīrti's instructions on these topics form the basis of what Tiantai doctrine refers to as the "perfect teaching five-gate dhyāna."

   In the *Sutra Spoken by Vimalakīrti*, Vimalakīrti is reported by Mahākatyāyāna to have taken issue with this śrāvaka's understanding of these five topics by saying, "Katyāyāna, don't employ a practice based in the mind subject to production and extinction to describe the dharmas of ultimate reality. Katyāyāna, dharmas are ultimately neither produced nor destroyed. This is the meaning of 'impermanence.' The five aggregates, when one completely penetrates through to their emptiness, are [seen to be] devoid of any arising. This is the meaning of 'suffering.' All dharmas are ultimately devoid of any [inherent] existence. This is the meaning of 'emptiness.' As for 'self' and 'non-self,' they are non-dual. This is the meaning of 'non-self.' Since dharmas are originally not as one perceives them, then they do not now undergo any cessation. This is the meaning of 'quiescent cessation.'" (See 維摩詰所說經 – T14.475.541a.)
8. According to the Sarvāstivādin *Mahā-vibhāṣa* by Vasumitra, this refers to the four dhyānas and the first three of the formless absorptions ("limitless space," "limitless consciousness," and "nothing whatsoever"). That Abhidharma commentary indicates that the bhikshu may rely on these seven absorptions in the process of severing the outflow-impurities (T27.1545.929b).
9. The nine sequential absorptions refers to the four dhyānas, the four formless absorptions, and the absorption involving extinction of the feeling and perception aggregates which is otherwise known as the "extinction" absorption (*nirodha-samāpatti*). (See *Foguang Dictionary*: 134; 5509.)
10. These are explained in the *Tiantai Bodhisattva Precepts Commentary* as the ten distinct component factors occurring in the four dhyānas. Although, when discussing each dhyāna individually, they total eighteen, if one considers them in the aggregate, eliminating all redundancies, there are ten according to this commentary. In fact, this would seem to contradict the analytic schemas of both Vasubandhu and Vasumitra which come up with a list of eleven by assigning the bliss of the third dhyāna to the feeling aggregate and the bliss of the first two dhyānas to the compositional-factors aggregate.

In any case, the Tiantai explanation is as follows: In the first dhyāna, there are five: initial ideation (*vitarka*), mental discursion (*vicāra*), joy (*prīti*), bliss (*sukha*), and single-minded concentration (*samādhi*). In the second dhyāna, there are four: inward purity (*saṃprasāda*), joy, bliss, and single-mindedness (of which the last three are redundant). In the third dhyāna, there are five: equanimity (*upekṣa*), mindfulness (*smṛti*), knowing awareness (*saṃprajñāna*), bliss, and single-mindedness (of which the last two are redundant). In the fourth dhyāna, there are four: neither suffering nor bliss (*aduḥka-asukha*), equanimity, mindfulness, and single-mindedness (of which the last three are redundant). (See 天台菩薩戒疏 – T40.1812.599b.)

11. The sixteen practice-aspects (*ṣoḍaśākārāḥ*) of the four truths: For the truth of suffering, we have impermanence (*anitya*), suffering (*duḥkha*), emptiness of inherent existence (*śūnya*), and non-self (*anātman*); for the truth of origination, we have causality (*hetu*), origination (*samudaya*), productivity (*prabhava*), and conditionality (*pratyaya*); for the truth of cessation, we have cessation (*nirodha*), tranquility (*śānta*), sublimity (*praṇīta*), and abandonment (*niḥsaraṇa*); and for the truth of the path, we have the existence of a path (*mārga*), its accordance with reality (*nyāya*), its progression (*pratipad*), and the fact that it leads forth (*nairyāṇika*). I derive the Sanskrit for these from *Foguang Dictionary* (387–8). My rendering of *praṇīta as* "sublime" finds agreement in Conze (*Materials for a Dictionary of the Prajñāpāramitā Literature*: 271).
12. This is a nearly exact quote from Kumārajīva's translation of Harivarman's *Satyasiddhi-śāstra* (T32.1646.373a). The more precise rendering would be: "Nirvāṇa is the true Dharma jewel. It is entered through many different gates." (泥洹是真法寶。以種種門入。)

Chapter One

1. *Taisho* reads "stations possessed of permanence." But this makes no sense at all and is obviously a corruption of the text which, as is quite clear from the context, should read "stations possessed of thought."
2. See *Foguang Dictionary* (p. 1200) for a relatively extensive explanation of the five wheel samādhis. It in turn refers us to Zhiyi's *Explanation of the Sequential Realization of the Dharma Gateways of Dhyāna Pāramitā*. (See 釋禪波羅蜜次第法門 – T46.1916.493b–c.)
3. The five: humans, gods, śrāvaka disciples, pratyekabuddhas, bodhisattvas. The more complete rendition counts seven such provisional-teaching practitioners by distinguishing three categories among the bodhisattva provisional-teaching practitioners. These classifications are correlated by the famous analogy of the "Medicinal Herbs" chapter of the *Lotus Sutra* with the various species of grasses, shrubs, and trees which all equally derive benefit from the rain. All of this relies on an analogy for the equal benefit brought to all classes of beings by the compassionate rain of the Buddha's teaching. (See *Foguang Dictionary*: 603; 6696.)
4. *Taisho* repeatedly employs a somewhat unorthodox alternate short-form transcription of the character *hui* (惠) which means "kindness" (ignored throughout this translation) for the obviously intended character *hui* (慧) which means "wisdom." The intended character is obvious from context and also corroborated by precise quotations of this passage in other works of the Tiantai tradition which employ the more standard "wisdom" character.
5. One will notice that a textual corruption has introduced a redundant listing of the eight liberations under an alternate Chinese translation alias typical of later periods in the history of Sino-Buddhist translation. *Ba beishe* (八背捨) was used earlier; *ba jietuo* (八解脫) eventually superceded it.
6. There does not seem to be any perfectly satisfactory translation for all of the Buddhist uses of the Sanskrit (*vivartanā*) or its Pali equivalent. The range of use in this text and in the early Indian Buddhist antecedents of this six-gate meditation tradition appears to be confined mainly to: "turning," "turning around," "turning back," "returning," and "changing." (See *Monier-Williams*: 988c.)
7. The *Taisho* text uses the *xiang* (想) which means "thought" instead of the *xiang* (相) which means "sign" or "mark." This is an obvious textual corruption corrected in this translation.

Chapter Two

1. A *kṣaṇa* is a fraction of an instant. It is variously defined as enduring for a sixtieth of a finger snap, a ninetieth of a "thought-moment", or one four-thousand, five-hundredth of a minute.
2. "Feeling" (*vedanā,* third among the five "aggregates," second among the five omnipresent mental factors) refers to six categories of direct sensory reception as it occurs at each of the six sense gates (eye, ear, nose, tongue, body, intellectual mind). As it occurs at the sixth sense gate (*mānas,* "intellectual mind"), this should not be confused with the discriminatory perception characteristic of the fourth aggregate and the fourth omnipresent mental factor (*saṃjñā,* "perceptive thought").
3. This is a direct quote from the *Heart Sutra.*
4. This "direct experiencing" is a compound used by particular translators to produce a Chinese-language rendering of the Sanskrit terms *samādhi* and *samāpatti.* It alludes to an absence of erroneous mental factors such as discursive thought and also refers to the "directness" of experience characteristic of meditative absorption.
5. The "five categories of skillful means" refers to twenty-five factors in five categories involved in the traditional Indian Buddhist cultivation and realization of calming-and-insight (*śamatha-vipaśyanā*).

   As recorded by Master Zhiyi's Tiantai teaching tradition, they include: 1) the fulfillment of five requisite conditions (purity in implementation of ethical precepts; adequacy of robes and food; a quiet place free of disturbances; relinquishment of responsibilities; proximity to a good spiritual guide); 2) the renunciation of the five desires (forms, sounds, smells, tastes, and touchables); 3) Elimination of the five hindrances (*nīvaraṇa*) or "coverings" (*āvaraṇa*) (sensual desire, ill-will, lethargy-and-sleepiness, excitedness-and-regretfulness, and doubt); 4) adjustment of five factors (mind, body, breath, sleep, food); and 5) practice of five dharmas (zeal, vigor, mindfulness, discernment, single-mindedness).

   For a complete explanation of these factors, see the third chapter of Master Zhiyi's *Essentials for Practicing Calming-and-Insight and Dhyāna Meditation.*

Chapter Three

1. The *Taisho* text reflects an obvious scribal error wherein *xin* (心) has been mistakenly substituted for *zhi* (止). The context makes it abundantly clear that the *zhi* is the correct character. I have incorporated the emendation in the translation (550c02).
2. As for: "Once one has realized this, one no longer simply accepts it," this means that one ceases to persist in uncritically "taking it on" or "subscribing to it" as a reflection of ultimate reality. One instead steps completely out of the duality-based conceptual construct through the skillful implementation of "turning" to look directly into the mind itself.
3. I happened to recognize this as a quote from Nāgārjuna's *Mahāprajnāpāramitā Upadeśa,* but with a textual corruption in which *xiang* (相) has been erroneously substituted for *xiang* (想), thus altering the meaning, but only slightly (T25.1509.190c). This translation reflects the original *Upadeśa* text, the context of which is a very long verse in praise of the perfection of wisdom.

Chapter Four

1. In the Sino-Buddhist commentarial tradition, the use of the term "noumenon" (*li* – 理) is as a reference to "ultimate truth" which is employed in contrast to "phenomena" (*shi* – 事), a reference to "conventional truth." "Noumenon" is synonymous with the "ultimate reality," or "suchness," realized only by the awakened mind. "Phenomena" is synonymous with the deceptive appearances of the worldly existence which so completely fool the minds of any who have not directly perceived their emptiness of inherent existence.

   Although, on the face of it, it might seem unfortunate to fall into the use of Kantian metaphysical terms as analogues for a more truly transcendent Buddhist concept, the Kantian use of the term is as a referent to "thing-in-itself," defined in *Webster's Third New International Dictionary* as "an ultimate reality unqualified by the subjective modes of human perception and thought." So, without suggesting that Kant ever truly understood (much less directly experienced) emptiness in the Nāgārjunian sense, still, the correspondence of definitions seems at least minimally adequate to function as a serviceable translation for the "*li-shi*," two-truths dichotomy of Chinese Buddhist metaphysical terminology.

2. "Two Vehicles" refers to: 1) the "Śrāvaka Disciples," those who gain arhat-level awakening through hearing the fundamental teachings of the Buddha; and 2) the Pratyekabuddhas, those who, in the absence of a Buddha, have gained a level of liberative awakening through the contemplation of causality. The awakening of a pratyekabuddha is itself of two classes. In one case, it corresponds to a lesser level of arhat enlightenment, and in another, it exceeds the awakening of even the most liberated arhat.

3. The delusions of "the four dwelling stations" refers to four categories of delusions operative within the three realms which manifest in the form of views and subtle thought. From coarsest to most subtle, they are: 1) All view-related delusions operative throughout the three realms; 2) All thought-related delusions operative within the desire realm. Among them, desire itself is most prominent. Hence they are given the designation "affections associated with desire"; 3) All thought-related delusions operative in the form realm. These are given the designation "form-related affections"; and 4) All thought-related delusions operative in the formless realm. These are given the designation "affections associated with existence." This per *Foguang Dictionary*: 1691b; 2996b.

4. I have preferred to reconstruct rather than translate the character used by the Sino-Buddhist tradition to translate the Sanskrit *ārya*

(*sheng* – 聖). Why? I find the two default English renderings and a more recent and slightly innovative rendering all to be untenable:

The first default translation, "sage," merely implies worldly wisdom. Much of what has been written by the so-called "sages" of both Eastern and Western philosophical history is, in Buddhist terms, classic "wrong view." There is almost no possibility that any of the identified "sages" of those traditions ever succeeded in realizing "the path of seeing" wherein one directly perceives the emptiness of inherent existence of all phenomena. Hence, by definition, none of these sages could likely have been an *ārya.*

The second default translation, "saint," has already been long assigned to states of extreme "holiness" as defined by Christian culture. Such "saints," although often noteworthy for consistently "selfless" behavior, are not particularly noted for the deep supramundane gnosis and wisdom which comes with the path of seeing defining an *ārya.*

Recently, some have chosen "superior" as a translation. As a standard term of reference for senior clerics in Catholic monasteries and convents, it seems to fall far short of the transcendent connotations of *ārya.*

5. Three poisons: greed (broadly defined as to include all types and degrees of attachment and desire); hatred; delusion.
6. The "ten agents" are comprised of five "sharp" agents (greed, hatred, delusion, arrogance, doubt) and five "dull" agents (the body-as-self view, extreme views, erroneous views, seizing-on-a-view views, seizing-on-rules-for-their-own-sake views). They are also known as "the ten great delusions" and as "the ten root delusions." See *Ding Fubao Buddhist Dictionary*: 238a, 1514a; *Foguang Dictionary*: 301b, 1164b.
7. "Primary ideation" or, alternately, just "ideation" (*vitarka*) corresponds to initial ideation whereas mental discursion (*vicāra*) corresponds to the subsequent stream of rumination on that topic which first arose with the primary ideation. A common analogy for these two: The loud sound which comes from the initial striking of a bell (primary ideation); The extended and progressively more subtle sound tones which ensue for a short while thereafter (mental discursion).
8. These nine contemplations visualize a corpse in nine different stages of deterioration, decomposition, and scattering.
9. The first two of the eight liberations are concerned with banishing both inwardly-based and outwardly-based sensual desire.
10. The topics involved in the eight bases of ascendancy are basically the same as with the eight liberations with the additional factor that, in the case of the bases of ascendancy, one completely conquers desires

and thus becomes invulnerable to further disturbance thereby.

11. "Other methods for the realization of 'impurity'" would include the contemplation of the thirty-two or thirty-six primary constituents of the body and also the progressively-developed contemplation of the white-boned skeleton.
12. One may interpret that what is intended here by "three emptinesses" is "the three gates to liberation" (emptiness, signlessness, wishlessness), this because "three emptinesses" is an alternate designation for those three types of samādhi. Still, it is perhaps equally likely that Master Zhiyi intends to refer here to the three emptinesses he pointed to earlier in this same work (at the very end of the second chapter), namely: the emptiness of beings, the emptiness of dharmas associated with reality, and uniform emptiness (550b18–19).
13. The Tiantai hermeneutic system refers to three types of purity ("purity associated with the provisional," "perfect purity," "purity of the fundamental nature") which are correlated with the three bodies of the Buddha, with three levels at which nirvāṇa manifests, with "three truths" (emptiness, the conventional, and the middle), and so forth.
14. See previous endnote.
15. See above two endnotes.
16. There is no such list digitally searchable in the *Taisho* canon. This is probably an aggregate reference to shorter lists of obstacles such as the various lists of "five obstacles" and the list of "ten obstacles" cut off by the bodhisattva on the ten grounds.
17. The three clarities (*jñāna-sākṣāt-kriya-vidyā*) refer to direct knowledge of past lives (*pūrva-nivāsānusmṛti*), the completely developed acuity of the heavenly eye to observe the continuum of a person's births and deaths (*cyuty-upapatti*), and direct knowledge of the destruction of outflow-impurities (*āsrava-kṣaya*). See *Foguang Dictionary*: 1290.
18. *Lotus Sutra* (T9.262.4c).

Chapter Five

1. As also occurred above at line 550c02, *Taisho* preserves an obvious scribal error here where the character *xin* (心) has been mistakenly substituted for the graphically similar *zhi* (止). I have emended the text accordingly and reflected the correction in the translation (551c12).
2. "Discerning wisdom" is a reference to the fourth of a list of "five practices" or "five skillful means" essential in conquest of the dhyānas. The complete list of five: zeal (*chanda*); vigor (*vīrya*); mindfulness (*smṛti*); discernment (*saṃprajñāna*); and single-mindedness (*citta-eka-agra*). Of course, even this list of five still only represents only a fifth of the comprehensive set of twenty-five factors considered necessary by the Buddhist tradition for acquisition of the dhyānas. (Refer back to the notes to Chapter Two.)

   These factors are discussed at length in the fifth chapter of Zhiyi's *Essentials for Practicing Calming-and-Contemplation and Dhyāna Meditation* and in the fourth chapter of *Nāgārjuna on the Six Perfections.*

Chapter Six

1. Error in Cbeta edition substitutes *ceng* (曾) for *hui* (會). *Taisho* and the Jin-ling woodblock both preserve the correct glyph (552b1).
2. The four types of feeling (*vedanā*) are determined on the basis of the realm inhabited by the experiencer of the feeling: 1) That which is connected to the desire realm; 2) That which is connected to the form realm; 3) That which is connected to the formless realm; and 4) That which is "unconnected." This per *Foguang Dictionary*: 3097b.
3. The four practice-aspects of the truth of suffering are: impermanence (*anitya*), suffering (*duḥkha*), emptiness of inherent existence (*śūnya*), and non-self (*anātman*).
4. The five "dull" agents are: the body-as-self view, extreme views, erroneous views, seizing-on-a-view views, seizing-on-rules-for-their-own-sake views.
5. The five "sharp" agents are: covetousness, hatred, delusion, arrogance, doubt.
6. As for this "having reached its end, one does not engage in the creation of anything new beyond that," it would seem to be primarily a reference to the utter finality of an arhat's nirvāṇa which involves a complete disinclination to pursue the altruistic path exemplified by the Buddha and the Bodhisattvas. On the most simple and obvious level, it may simply be a reference to the absence of any further karmic activity of any kind.
7. This is a slightly paraphrased quotation from the *Mahāparinirvāṇa Sutra*. A more literal unparaphrased translation would be: "It is analogous to the case of the grasses and trees on the banks of a river which are all swept away into the great sea by the torrential currents of a massive flood—all, with the sole exception of the willow [which remains] on account of its pliancy. Son of good family, all beings are just like this. In every case, they all follow along with the current and enter the sea of death. [This is the case for] all of them, with the sole exception of the bodhisattva who abides in the great *parinirvāṇa* of the Great Vehicle." (See T12.374.437b.)
8. Per treatises attributed to Nāgārjuna, when the bodhisattva enters the "bodhisattva position" (*bodhisattvaniyāma*), this coincides with the realization of the unproduced-dharmas patience (*anutpattikadharma-kṣānti*) and attainment of the irreversibility of the *avaivartika* whose future realization of buddhahood is no longer in the slightest doubt.

Chapter Seven

1. "All of the practices" likely refers to the ten thousand practices typical of the bodhisattva's path to buddhahood whereas "meritorious-quality characteristics" likely refers to the thirty-two marks and eighty subsidiary characteristics generated thereby in the body of a buddha.
2. "Delusive ignorance (*avidyā*) is the first of the "links" in the twelve-fold chain of causes and conditions.
3. The six "obstructive conditions" (*ṣaḍ-vipakṣa*) are the six types of mind most likely to interfere with development of the six perfections. In order, they are: the mind of covetousness (interferes with giving); the mind inclined to break moral precepts (interferes with moral virtue); the mind of hatefulness (interferes with patience); the mind of indolence (interferes with vigor); the scattered mind (interferes with dhyāna meditation); the deluded mind (interferes with wisdom). This list is discussed by Nāgārjuna in *Mahāprajnāpāramitā Upadeśa* (T12.1509.303c–4b).
4. The *Taisho* edition incorporates an obvious graphic-similarity scribal error (惱) in place of the obviously intended word for "covetousness" (慳). The Jinling woodblock preserves the correct version which I incorporate here in the English translation (553b18).
5. In *Taisho*, there is an interpolated four-character phrase (即便之心) which appears to be a corruption-by-interpolation. Although, based on other editions, it appears to be an interpolation, I do go ahead and translate it in parentheses. I prefer here the reading of other editions (including the Jinling woodblock) which do not reflect this apparent interpolation (553b22).

Chapter Eight

1. "Great root faculties" refers here to highly developed spiritual faculties established through many lifetimes of engaging in the bodhisattva practices.
2. For those unfamiliar with the technical terms, a brief explanation of "mind king" and "mental-factor dharmas" is in order. The "mind king" is the subjective aspect of the mind. "Mental factor dharmas" or, more simply, just "mental factors," is a reference to the dharmas belonging to the mind (*caitasika-dharma*). These latter include fifty-one mental factors (per classic 100-dharma schema of Vasubandhu). These fifty-one mental factors are in turn broken down into six subcategories:

   1) The "universally-functioning mental factors" [mental contact at the level of the intellectual mind faculty, mental sensation, etc.];

   2) The "object-ascertaining mental factors" [zeal, decisive understanding, recollection, etc.];

   3) The "good mental factors" [faith, sense of shame, dread of blame, absence of covetousness, etc.];

   4) The "major afflictions" [covetousness, hatred, delusion, arrogance, etc.];

   5) The "subsidiary afflictions" [anger, enmity, concealment, etc.];

   6) The "indeterminate mental factors" [regret, drowsiness, initial ideation; mental discursion].
3. The ten destinies are: the hells, *pretas* (hungry ghosts, etc.), animals, humans, *asuras* (demi-gods or "titans"), celestial beings or "gods," arhats, pratyekabuddhas, bodhisattvas, and buddhas. Because a highly-evolved bodhisattva can actually manifest for beings as a fully-enlightened buddha, the reference may be to the "other" nine destinies in addition to the one in which the bodhisattvic practitioner is already manifesting.
4. One will notice once again Master Zhiyi's multiple approaches to explaining the concept of "turning / turning back." Not only does he make it refer primarily to the duality-transcending turning back from duality-based perceptions of objective realms to contemplate the mind itself, but he also employs the term to refer secondarily to the bodhisattva's turning back from directly contemplating the mind to engage the world and work therein for the liberation of beings.
5. The latter half of the quote is found in the *Bejeweled Cloud Sutra* (寶雲經). The first line may be paraphrasing a line from later in the scripture (T16.658.211a, 230b).

Chapter Nine

1. *Taisho* has "nonexistent" (無) here, which makes no sense and appears to be an obvious scribal error. I have preferred the "sublime" (妙) of other editions such as the Jin-ling woodblock (554b8).
2. This is a citation from the tenth chapter of the *Lotus Sutra* (T09.262.31c).
3. Ibid. T09.278.449c.

Chapter Ten

1. In his *Explanation of the Sequential Stages in the Dharma Gateway of Dhyāna Pāramitā* (釋禪波羅蜜次第法門 – T46.1916.510a–b), Zhiyi lists two sets of eight which he adds together to give the sixteen: movement, itching, coolness, warmth, lightness, heaviness, roughness, slipperiness, agitation, softness, coldness, heat, floating, sinking, hardness, pliancy.
2. The practitioner should realize that the meditation states listed here are for the most part not inherently positive developments. In fact, if attached to as in any way ultimate or desirable, they may very likely throw one off of the path of right Dharma entirely. They are listed here simply because they are extremely common experiences more-or-less characteristic of the beginning practitioner's initial attempts to cultivate the first of the six gates.
3. The phrase "...and the others on through to" here refers to the standard "nine reflections on the unlovely" which involve meditation on the nine different states in which a deteriorating corpse may be found.

   The "white skeleton which radiates light" is a reference to the white-boned skeleton when contemplated in the context of this nine-fold schema or, alternately, when contemplated in the context of a specific serially-generated set of visualizations of the skeleton within one's own body and then of skeletons filling up even all of empty space. The latter context is, in and of itself, a classic meditation exercise narrated in great detail in the sutra canon.
4. This is a reference to the mention at the beginning of this sub-section on "interrelated signs" of the relevance of topics contained in chapters three thru six, with the relevant section of the sixth chapter being limited to the contemplations held in common by all Three-Vehicles practitioners (554b19–21).
5. My translation of this very important and remarkably detailed classic meditation manual by Master Zhiyi is entitled the *Essentials of Buddhist Meditation*.

6. The *Taisho* edition of the text records an obvious scribal error (說) in place of the graphically-similar original (證) preserved in other editions. This English translation corrects the error (554c20).
7. The *Taisho* edition records what is clearly a scribal error (利) in place of the graphically-similar original (別) preserved in other editions. The correction is reflected in this English translation (555a26).
8. Here as in some other points in this translation, I have preferred to reconstruct the Sanskrit for pratyekabuddha in preference to indulging a rather clumsy English rendering of the Chinese "enlightened via conditions."
9. An "ineffable" is actually a traditional Indian number.
10. As quoted, this passage finds a perfect match only in the *Humane King Prajñāpāramitā Sutra* (佛說仁王般若波羅蜜經 – T08.245.827b). "Three levels of worthies" refers to the bodhisattvas engaged in cultivation of the ten dwellings, the ten practices, and the ten transferences. As for the "ten levels of āryas," this refers to the bodhisattvas on the ten grounds (*bhūmi*).
11. T09.262.5c.
12. This is a reference to the 27-fascicle *Mahāprajñāpāramitā Sutra* (T08.223.256a–b?). I haven't located the precise citation. The general discussion which concludes with a roughly corresponding statement is found at 256a-b.
13. T12.374.590a.
14. T09.278.395b.
15. T09.262.5c.

About the Translator

Bhikshu Dharmamitra (ordination name "Heng Shou" – 釋恆授) is a Chinese-tradition translator-monk and one of the early American disciples (since 1968) of the late Weiyang Ch'an patriarch, Dharma teacher, and exegete, the Venerable Master Hsuan Hua (宣化上人). He has a total of 23 years in robes during two periods as a monastic (1969–1975; 1991 to present).

Dharmamitra's principal educational foundations as a translator lie in four years of intensive monastic training and Chinese-language study of classic Mahāyāna texts in a small-group setting under Master Hua from 1968–1972, undergraduate Chinese language study at Portland State University, a year of intensive one-on-one Classical Chinese study at the Fu Jen University Language Center near Taipei, and two years at the University of Washington's School of Asian Languages and Literature (1988–90).

Since taking robes again under Master Hua in 1991, Dharmamitra has devoted his energies primarily to study and translation of classic Mahāyāna texts with a special interest in works by Ārya Nāgārjuna and related authors. To date, he has translated a dozen important texts, most of which are slated for publication by Kalavinka Press.

Kalavinka Buddhist Classics Title List

Meditation Instruction Texts

The Essentials of Buddhist Meditation

A marvelously complete classic *śamathā-vipaśyanā* (calming-and-insight) meditation manual. By Tiantai Śramaṇa Zhiyi (538–597 CE).

The Six Gates to the Sublime

The earliest Indian Buddhist meditation method explaining the essentials of breath and calming-and-insight meditation. By Śramaṇa Zhiyi.

Bodhisattva Path Texts

Nāgārjuna on the Six Perfections

Chapters 17–30 of Ārya Nāgārjuna's *Mahāprājñāpāramitā Upadeśa.*

Marvelous Stories from the Perfection of Wisdom

130 stories from Ārya Nāgārjuna's *Mahāprājñāpāramitā Upadeśa.*

A Strand of Dharma Jewels (Ārya Nāgārjuna's *Ratnāvalī*)

The earliest extant edition, translated by Paramārtha: *ca* 550 CE

Nāgārjuna's Guide to the Bodhisattva Path

The *Bodhisaṃbhāra Treatise* with abridged Vaśitva commentary.

The Bodhisaṃbhāra Treatise Commentary

The complete exegesis by the Indian Bhikshu Vaśitva (*ca* 300–500 CE).

Letter from a Friend - The Three Earliest Editions

The earliest extant editions of Ārya Nāgārjuna's *Suhṛlekkha*:

Translated by Tripiṭaka Master Guṇavarman (*ca* 425 CE)
Translated by Tripiṭaka Master Saṅghavarman (*ca* 450 CE)
Translated by Tripiṭaka Master Yijing (*ca* 675 CE)

Resolve-for-Enlightenment Texts

On Generating the Resolve to Become a Buddha

On the Resolve to Become a Buddha by Ārya Nāgārjuna
Exhortation to Resolve on Buddhahood by Patriarch Sheng'an Shixian
Exhortation to Resolve on Buddhahood by the Tang Literatus, Peixiu

Vasubandhu's Treatise on the Bodhisattva Vow

By Vasubandhu Bodhisattva (*ca* 300 CE)

*All Kalavinka Press translations include facing-page source text.

CPSIA information can be obtained
at www.ICGtesting.com
Printed in the USA
BVHW030224040720
582943BV00002B/313